This publication is the product of a FÁS training project administered by the Croagh Patrick Archaeological Committee. FÁS projects are funded by the exchequer, the European Union Social Fund and the local community.

Published by
The Croagh Patrick Archaeological Committee, Westport, Co. Mayo.

D1471193

First published by the Croagh Patrick Archaeological Committee in 2001.

British Library Cataloguing in Publication Data
ISBN – O 9536086-3-8

Foreword

The publication of this book comes at a time when all parts of Ireland are undergoing change. This change which is primarily due to our newly acquired prosperity, has gripped the country in nearly every aspect of life, while we as a nation have moved further away from the land and are adopting modern technology, in whatever form that takes. Although in the Westport-Murrisk--Liscarney and surrounding areas, farming is still practised, the housing expansion so vigorous nationwide is everywhere evident. Certainly were that not the case in the midst of the current prosperity, we would have cause for concern. However, as will be seen through this book, such dramatic change is not new to Ireland. The exceptionally large population before and during the Famine times in the 19th century may never be repeated, and topographical evidence from this period exists in the scores of lazy beds or cultivation ridges on the foothills and lower ground around Croagh Patrick. Similarly, the arrival of Christianity to these shores appears to have coincided with a significant increase in the population and an associated mushrooming of the ubiquitous ringfort from that time. Situated as we are on the threshold of a new millennium, it can be a useful exercise to identify our position in the evolution of our place and its people. By looking at surviving monuments and identifying place names, we may start to envisage the lives and landscapes of those who preceded us. These indications are all about us. It is my hope that this book will provide the reader, be they local amateur enthusiast, professional archaeologist or visitor, with the necessary language to better understand and appreciate our – small in size but large in spirit – Croagh Patrick area.

Contents

Contents: continued

Acknowledgements

Compliments and gratitude are extended to FÁS as the primary sponsors and facilitators of the project. A particular and personal thank you to Mr Jackie Foley, Senior Training Officer with FÁS (Castlebar) and Mr Harry Hughes (Chairman, Croagh Patrick Archaeological Committee, Westport), who nursed the project along gently and unobtrusively. I also extend my thanks to all members of the Croagh Patrick Archaeological Committee, and especially to all the landowners for their interest, understanding and tolerance of our activities. Many locals allowed us, even invited us, into their homes to recount valuable folklore material and we and future generations are indebted to you. Additional thanks to Mr Ian Williams who directed the survey during my absence and who helped in the preparation of the catalogue; Gerry Walsh, Castlebar, for permission to summarise his excavations on the summit of Croagh Patrick and to reproduce some of the finds here; Rose Cleary for access to her report on the glass beads from the same Croagh Patrick excavations; Christiaan Corlett (Dúchas) for information from his files on the area and for his support and interest; Mary Tunney and S.M.R. staff who generously provided good quality copies of 1838-1844 O.S. maps; Mary Cahill of the National Museum who allowed access to the topographical files of the area, and also for her comments on gold and gold mining; Eamon Coady (Dúchas, and formerly of the Megalithic Survey) for his help and advice; Declan Little of the Department of Environmental Resource Management U.C.D. for his help, interest and advice – Declan, along with Mr McGee, Mitchell and von Engelbrechten, kindly allowed me access to their recent Palaeoecological study from Brackloon Wood (see bibliography); the staff at Mayo County Library and GMIT, Castlebar; those in the Roads Section, Áras an Chondae who were all most helpful to me; Claire Cotter (Discovery Programme) for her considerable help in the layout of the book, her suggestions and advice; Owen Campbell, Murrisk, for copies of old maps and for challenging questions; Gerry Bracken, Westport, for permission to include a summary account of his article on the Rolling Sun theory; Ines Hagen (Discovery Programme) who allowed us access to her thesis which she carried out in the Killadangan townland area; Kevin Barton (Applied Geophysics Unit N.U.I.G.) and Louise Geraghty for help in the preparation of the geology of the area; Barry Masterson (Dublin) for preparation and publication of the distribution maps; the clergy of the parish and particularly to Fr O'Connor whose concern for Oughavale graveyard helped keep it so tidy; Donal Mac Giolla Easpaig (Irish Placenames Commission) for help with the chapter on local placenames; Christine Grant and Amanda Loughran for access to their excavation reports on a hut site in Glenbaun, and permission to include some of the findings here. Thanks also to Michael Moore (Dúchas), Gerry Walsh, Harry Hughes, Michael Gibbons, Jarlath Duffy, Olive Alcock and especially to Elizabeth Farrell for help with proof reading. My gratitude to the Geological Survey of Ireland for permission to use local geology map; the National Library for 1791 drawing of Murrisk Friary and the Ordnance Survey Office, Dublin for permission to reproduce a section of the 1840 map. Also thanks to Robert Kilkelly and Associates, Angela Gallagher, Galway and Catherine Roughneen, Meelick, Swinford for their help. For providing photographs used in the book, I would like to thank Harry Hughes, Siobhán Duffy, Gerry Bracken, Christiaan Corlett, Gerry Walsh, Michael O'Sullivan, Richard Gillespie, Ian Williams, Frank Dolan, Keith Heneghan, Noel O'Neill and Tom Campbell, Castlebar. A special word of thanks and appreciation to all those who worked on the survey in various capacities, especially to Martina O'Kane (Co-ordinator) for her patience, her diligence to the cause and her support over the years; and to David Loftus (draughtsperson) and Siobhán Duffy (chief photographer) for their willingness to help in those post-fieldwork, pre-publication days. All the sites visited and recorded in the book appear here through the diligence and interest of the following survey team:

DIRECTORS:
Leo Morahan
Ian Williams

CO-ORDINATORS:
Martina O'Kane
David Loftus
Richard Gillespie
Gillian McCarthy

FIELD WORKERS:

Siobhán Duffy	Carole Killeen
Patricia Kilcoyne	Dwayne Jordan
Aileen Moloney	Ted Walsh
John Chambers	Rowena Keane
Justin Fitzgerald	John Flanagan
Pat McDonagh	Mary Ellen Kilbane
Sean MacNally	Paul Clarke
Noel Fahy	Gráinne Byrne
Reg Roynan	Jean McGrane
Rosa Meehan	Will Igoe
Eileen Kavanagh	Honora Broderick

Finally, I would like to acknowledge the help, support and patience of Joan King during field work and in the pre-publication days.

Go raibh maith agaibh go léir.

Leo Morahan
Director, Croagh Patrick Archaeological Survey

Preface

Croagh Patrick Archaeological Committee

Croagh Patrick is Ireland's oldest continuous Christian pilgrimage extending over 1,500 years. The mountain is now renowned for its annual pilgrimage on the last Sunday of July. This, and its historical and archaeological abundance, make it Ireland's most climbed mountain; and evidence from the archaeological surveys suggests that the summit was visited for many years even before St. Patrick's pilgrimage. It is appropriate that, as we enter the third millennium since the birth of Christ, the archaeological remains of the previous millennia should be recorded.

The Croagh Patrick Archaeological Committee was founded in 1994 to investigate the archaeological remains on Croagh Patrick. With support from Mayo County Council and its manager, Mr Des Mahon, the Committee appointed Mr Gerry Walsh as archaeological director. The first season's investigation uncovered the remains of an Early Christian oratory buried on the summit. This major discovery encouraged the Committee to form *Friends of Croagh Patrick* to help fund the second season. Many people joined the *Friends* and paid thirty pounds per year for three years. The second season's (1995) investigations uncovered a hilltop rampart enclosing the summit of the mountain and some glass beads of antiquity. A group of people including archaeologists Mr Gerry Walsh, Mr Michael Gibbons, and the Guardian of Croagh Patrick, Mr John Cummins, climbed to the summit each day for eight weeks to work on the excavations.

The Committee approached FÁS in 1996 to organise a full archaeological survey of the orbit of Croagh Patrick. Mr Jackie Foley from FÁS fully supported the project and under the direction of Mr Leo Morahan, archaeologist, a team of ten people surveyed the area for two years. Many new monuments and sites were discovered and recorded and this book is a testament to the dedication of the team and the survey director, Mr Leo Morahan.

The project has the full support and assistance of the Archbishop of Tuam, Dr Michael Neary and the former Archbishop, Dr Joseph Cassidy; the past parish administrators Canon Anthony King, Very Rev. Pádraig O'Connor, and the current administrator Very Rev. Michael Molloy.

I thank all those people who worked on the surveys, and those who contributed financially towards them. I also thank members of the Croagh Patrick Archaeological Committee for all their efforts. The Committee will work with local tourism bodies to gain benefit from this vast heritage for the local economy – which is already happening with the development of the National Famine Memorial and the Millennium Park at Murrisk.

This publication is important both nationally and locally. It will be an important source for local and national agencies and of value in education and conservation. It should encourage interest by locals and tourists in our heritage and its protection.

Harry Hughes
Chairman, Croagh Patrick Archaeological Committee

FÁS

My involvement with FÁS has taken me to all corners of Co. Mayo over the past two decades or so. Each project under our aegis has had its own unique ethos, with achievements forming positive steps in the evolution and growth of communities. It has been most fulfilling to be able to support the development of social and economic enterprises, which in turn I hope have benefitted the local economy and social regeneration.

I was delighted when in July 1996 I learned that the Croagh Patrick Archaeological Committee intended to carry out an archaeological survey of the area, and proud to have represented FÁS in the initial stages and throughout the course of the project. To me, the undertaking was a celebration of the richness of my own place, the area where I was born and spent most of my years – so any help I gave was a labour of love.

Initially, the team was put in place under the direction of Leo Morahan. Over the course of the survey, the group retained its professionalism, efficiency and dedication. Underlying this singlemindedness there was a vein of 'savvy', simple common sense, which helped overcome many obstacles and opened doors others might have baulked at.

As a Westport native, it has been exciting to see so many significant findings from the Croagh Patrick area, and to have them so well presented in this publication. In my position with FÁS, it has been a source of great fulfillment and pride to have helped in the establishment and running of the project. I wish every success to all those who worked on the survey over the years and to all members of the Croagh Patrick Archaeological Committee, who will now undoubtedly be moving on to further challenges.

Go n-eirí leo go léir.

Jackie Foley
Community Employment Officer, FÁS Castlebar

Mayo County Council

Is cuis mhór áthas dom mar Bhainisteoir Chomhairle Chontae Mhaigh Éo fáilte a chur roimh an bhfóilseachán tábhachtacht seo.

Rising 2,510 ft (765m) above sea level the beautiful mountain of Croagh Patrick, overlooking Clew Bay, has been a sacred mountain for over 5,000 years. St. Patrick spent 40 days and nights praying and fasting on the mountain in 441AD. Today Croagh Patrick remains Ireland's most important 'Holy Mountain' with up to 100,000 visitors annually. On a clear day the view from the top is spectacular. This area of immense beauty is a place dear to my own heart. I have firsthand experience of the tremendous community spirit of the people of this area. The village of Murrisk was chosen as the site for the National Famine Monument in 1997. This bronze sculpture by John Behan depicts a skeleton-strung famine ship evoking many victims of the Great Famine in Ireland. Recently the National Millennium Committee of Ireland awarded the Murrisk Development Association finance for the construction of a Millennium Park.

Murrisk has been awarded the Eco-Label in recognition of the fact that the area has an environment of high quality and a community committed to managing it in a suitable way. The village won the Waterside Village Award in the 1999 Irish Tidy Towns Competition, while Bertra Beach, located beside the village, has been awarded the EU Blue Flag.

Mayo County Council is pleased to have been involved in all of these achievements, so I have been intensely aware of the tremendous energy pouring from this area. This publication is a further example of this vitality. The Croagh Patrick Archaeological Committee has produced a unique social and archaeological record of Croagh Patrick·and its environment. A production of this complexity does not happen without the involvement of a great number of organisations and individuals. I extend congratulations to Director Leo Morahan, Chairman Harry Hughes and the other members of the Croagh Patrick Archaeological Committee. In addition, I wish to commend Jackie Foley and his FÁS workers and everyone involved in making this project a reality. Mayo County Council is delighted to be associated with this publication which celebrates the spiritual significance and sense of continuity of our own 'Holy Mountain' in a world of change.

When people speak of holy mountains or special places such as Kilimanjaro, Mount Fuji, Mount Everest, Croagh Patrick holds its own with the best of them for history, heritage, archaeology and adventure.

Des Mahon
Mayo County Manager

Chapter 1

Introduction and Background

1.1 This book is the result of an archaeological survey carried out in the general Croagh Patrick area between 1996 and 1998. Prior to the survey, attention was focused on the summit of the mountain in 1994 and 1995 where archaeological excavations under the direction of Gerry Walsh uncovered the walls of an Early Christian oratory and remains of a drystone rampart wall which enclosed the summit of the Reek (as the mountain is known locally). A positive progression, it was felt, would be to record all antiquities in the general Croagh Patrick area. FÁS were approached for funding, sponsorship and general support, and responded favourably on all fronts. An official survey home was established in the Westport Boat Club, and fieldwork commenced in October 1996. Additional support and back-up was forthcoming from the Croagh Patrick Archaeological Committee. The Croagh Patrick Archaeological Committee, established in 1994, was primarily responsible for the commencement of the mountain top excavations. During the summer months of 1994 and 1995, a group of workers together with the director climbed the mountain each day, returning each evening following a full day's excavation (see excavation report p. 18-22).

1.2 Croagh Patrick is an imposing, pyramid-like quartzite mountain on the southern shores of Clew Bay, which rises to 765m and which dominates the landscape here in a magnificent and majestic manner. The busy tourist town of Westport guards the mouth of Clew Bay to the east, and travelling westwards from there by the northern edges of the mountain mass brings one to the small town of Louisburgh. Both towns are roughly equidistant from the village of Murrisk, from where the bulk of pilgrims and hillwalkers commence the ascent of Croagh Patrick. The survey area concentrated on the mountain block of Croagh Patrick and its associated hinterland, taking in several topographical archaeological zones; these range from the mountain top and its uplands to vast tracts of peatlands to the south, a large drumlin belt primarily to the east, with the coastal maritime zone forming the northern boundary of the surveyed area.

Apart from the coastal area and S of Westport town, all the ground is more than 60m above sea level. Initially it was hoped to extend the survey to the Erriff river valley, which forms the natural divide between this area and the Partry mountains, but we finally selected the Owenmore river to the S. This forms a major natural barrier between the Croagh Patrick range and the Sheeffry Hills and it eventually merges with the Erriff river. The western boundary, while it is roughly a division between high mountainy ground and lower pasture fields, is also the civil parish boundary between Oughavale and Kilgeever; Westport to the east is the chief town of the former while Louisburgh to the west is the service town, market place and educational centre for the latter. In the NE part, all the townlands in the Westport town catchment area to the S of the Carrowbeg river were surveyed, apart from Westport Demesne which contains Westport House, Estate and Golf Course and which straddles both sides of the river.

In terms of drainage, the Owenwee is the main river through the area; with its source on high ground to the SW of the Reek, it follows a circuitous route to enter the sea ENE of the mountain top in Belclare. Interestingly, its source is within 300m of one of the sources of the Bellakip river, which is a tributary of the Bunowen, one of the largest rivers running through Kilgeever parish to the west. Scores of other streams and rivulets originate on all slopes of the mountain range, creating in most instances permanent valley scars. Along the coast from Westport to

Louisburgh the T39 is the main communications route, with the N59 from Westport to Leenaun passing initially between numerous hills and drumlins, and ultimately following the Erriff river valley all the way to the Killary Harbour. Roads of varying standards serve most of the townlands, with one from Kilsallagh to Bouris serving Drummin and Liscarney, breaching the back, or southern side, of Croagh Patrick and forming the tightest possible road circuit of the mountain.

1.3 In carrying out the survey, the aim was to visit, identify and describe all known antiquities within the designated area. The catalogue in this book contains a brief description of each site – more detailed records of all sites were made, and these, together with accompanying plans and photographs, have been forwarded to the Record of Monuments and Places Office in Dublin, Mayo County Library, Castlebar and Westport Library. Within this publication, a select number of plans and photographs are used, the former showing at least one example of most types of antiquities from the list. As with all similar surveys from around Ireland, the cut-off date for archaeological monuments is 1700, though here a brief mention is given to some mills and lime kilns, which are thought to be later. The distribution maps help trace various phases of settlement and activity from the earliest times. Apart from the archaeological record, there is a collection of fifteen folklore interviews with local residents, many of which provided names used in the text, and are suggestive of the presence of still standing or former monuments. The Croagh Patrick Archaeological Survey is but one of a number which were carried out in Mayo during the past thirteen years, including Aghamore parish, Drum half parish (Belcarra area), the Kilmurry area near Crossmolina, the Irishtown-Ballindine area, a survey of the barony of Erris and the Mayo Abbey parish. In addition to these, a larger scale survey of eight O.S. 6˝ maps (six inches to one mile scale) was carried out in the Ballinrobe area from 1989 to 1992. In Turlough parish (new home of the Irish Folklife Collection), outside Castlebar, extensive fieldwork undertaken by Christy Lawless has led to the discovery of scores of fulacht fiadha; several students have over the years selected west Mayo and other parts of the county for specialised and detailed archaeological and historical research. Guarding the mouth of Clew Bay lies Clare Island, which is unquestionably the most surveyed of this country's offshore islands. Since the start of the twentieth century, surveys which embraced geology, zoology, folklore, botany and archaeology have been carried out. Most of the findings of this survey have been published with the expertise and financial help of The Royal Irish Academy. The most recent archaeological survey of Clare Island has been completed and is due to be published in the near future.

1.4 A brief layout of the book is presented here. Initially it deals with the lead-up to the initiation of the survey and follows this up with a look at the geographical area – how it is delimited, its main physical features, drainage and transport routes. This is followed by the aims and scope of the book and a mention of other field surveys which have been carried out in County Mayo. Chapter 2 takes a general look at the geography and geology of the area and concludes with a summary account of a recent (as yet unpublished) palaeoecological study carried out in Brackloon Wood and dating from c. 10,000 BP (before present).

Chapter 3 gives a summary account of the 1994-95 excavations on the mountain from an original report by Gerry Walsh. It also looks at relevant historical references to Croagh Patrick while treating briefly of St. Patrick, references to some local medieval buildings and artefacts and concludes with a mention of gold from the area.

All monuments from the survey are included in Chapter 4 and are found on one of the following 6˝ O.S. maps: 86, 87, 88, 96, 97 or 98 (Figs. 1a + 1b). Each site type is dealt with chronologically, with an introductory paragraph preceding each monument type. Subsequent

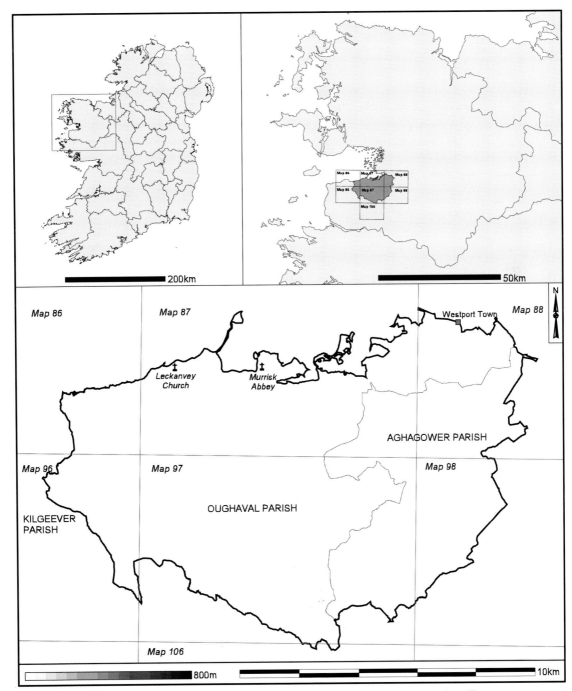

Fig. 1a: Location maps showing the region nationally and the survey area locally.

mention in text will refer to the monument's number in the Catalogue of Sites. Individual monuments under any classification type appear alphabetically under the townland name and numerically under the S.M.R. list for Co. Mayo. While the bulk of the catalogue is archaeological, some monuments near the end of the list are of more recent vintage.

Chapter 5 looks at the landscape of the monuments in prehistoric and later in historic times. This evolves into a discussion on the type of sites and their distribution and a look at comparable monuments either nationally or locally.

Chapter 6 looks at the townland and other local placenames, and attempts to give the origin for these names. In addition, all the monuments, placenames and buildings of interest from each of the townlands are included in this list.

People, and its use in the title embraces all our ancestors who through their imagination, labours, lives and deaths have helped create the wealth of monuments around us.

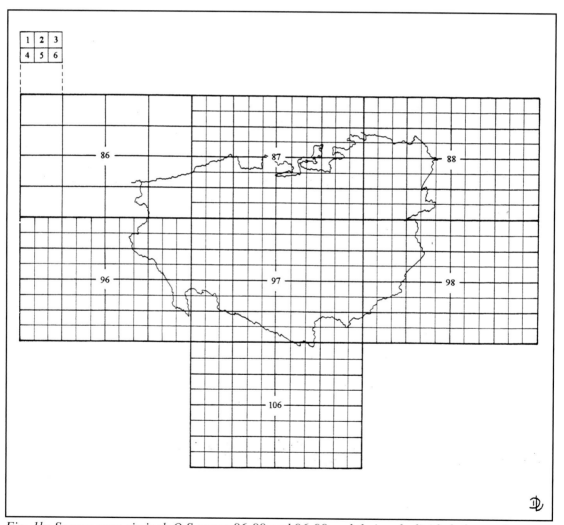

Fig. 1b: Survey area six inch O.S. maps 86-88 and 96-98 and their sub-divided plan and trace.

Chapter 2

Natural Landscape

2.1 Geography and Geology

The most noticeable physical attributes of the area include the mountainous nature of Croagh Patrick itself, the multitude of drumlins to be found within and outside Clew Bay, and the changing coastline of Clew Bay. Geologically and geographically, the area could justifiably term itself the gold coast. Firstly, pre-Devonian rocks at Croagh Patrick and Cregganbaun contain sites for gold mineralisation (McArdle 1989) with the gold apparently confined to quartz veins. The area was explored by Burmin Exploration and Development and the results showed that the veins contain approximately 170 grammes of gold per tonne of waste. Additionally, the southern side of Clew Bay contains miles of clean golden sandy beaches which are generally sheltered and unspoilt.

As an overview to the geology, the earth is thought to have formed 4,500 million years ago while the oldest known rocks are about 50 million years younger. The oldest rocks to have been found in Ireland date to 1,700 million years ago while those in Connemara and south Mayo have a geological history of 750 million years. Ireland's geological evolution has witnessed many diverse locations with the country or parts of it spending periods immersed in ancient oceans and other periods spent close to the equator, complete with tropical seas similar to the Bahamas of today.

During the last great glaciation to hit these shores (c. 10,000 years BC), gravelly earthen material deposited by the ice formed a plethora of drumlins and ridges, most noticeable to the north of a line from Galway Bay to Carlingford Lough. In the intervening millennia, the rising waters of Clew Bay are eating into many of the drumlins here; these form a remarkable archipelago most favourably viewed from Croagh Patrick to the south. Originally, these island drumlins extended farther out in Clew Bay but exposure to the rougher seas may have washed their upper sections away. Those that survive resemble large ski ramps in the bay, their outlines sloping gently eastwards with their more exposed seaward sides often formed by low yet steep cliffs.

The shores of Clew Bay are underlain by a Palaeozoic strata which includes old red sandstone and some carboniferous limestone. There is an extensive band of carboniferous limestone arcing eastwards from Westport, through Lough Carra, along by the east of Loughs Mask and Corrib towards Galway. Much of the older basement rock in the survey area is formed of schists, and among the most significant of these is the band of quartzite which is exposed on the top and northern shoulders of Croagh Patrick. A number of geological faults or localised rock formations have adapted local names, with examples such as The Letterbrock Formation, The Bouris Formation, The Killadangan Formation, The Lough Nacorra Formation and The Deer Park Complex. At the latter, the rocks which are metamorphosed include serpentine and talc carbonate schists. Around ten years ago, some tests were carried out locally to determine if talc was sufficiently plentiful to be extracted. Symes 1868 map shows serpentine exposed on the surface in Clerhaun townland. Close to the S of this location, a quarried area on the same map showed 'well bedded finely laminated quartzite used for flooring flags'. The residue from this activity is still present at the site today. The presence of gold together with serpentine and talc show the area to have been resource-rich for prehistoric peoples and highlights the mountain block as one of great potential for early settlers. An Early Bronze Age soap stone mould from talc carbonate was found in Culfin townland less than 20km to the SW at the mouth of Killary Harbour. Serpentine is the stone associated with Connemara marble and some serpentine beads have been uncovered at excavations in Lough Gur in Co. Limerick. Gold, as a resource, has been utilised since the Bronze Age and is evidenced in several early artefacts.

The geology of the area reflects itself in several of the archaeological monuments with nearly all of the standing stones and most of the cashel construction being of schist. Further glacial evidence is visible in some of the heavily dredged river valleys on the northern slopes of Croagh Patrick and the large natural amphitheatre or cirque NE of the summit, which today goes by the name of Lugnademon. As stated earlier, the area is serviced by an abundance of water with the mountain block forming the source of some large streams and smaller tributaries. Lough Nacorra on the southern end of Croagh Patrick appears originally to have been a much larger lake, which has been displaced over time by peat formation. In fact, the post-glacial interval has left its legacy in the form of extensive peat deposits over vast tracts to the S and W of the mountain. Some pine forests or woodland survived before the formation of much of the bog and the roots of some of these tree stumps are still embedded in the bedrock in Furgill and Lenanadurtaun townlands. A soil map of the area shows that, apart from peat, there are high occurrences of gleys and podsols. Gleys are the product of waterlogged soil conditions while the soil profile of podsols is formed at an advanced stage of leaching (or removal of soil material in solution).

2.2 The Evolution of Brackloon Wood

Introduction

In the aftermath of the last ice age (c. 12,000 years ago), much of Ireland and particularly the northern half would have been an inhospitable place for the generation of any plant or tree growth. Eventually, the establishment of trees and other plants permitted colonisation by animals and subsequently by man, where earlier neither could have survived in cold barren conditions. Mount Sandel in Northern Ireland has revealed evidence of occupation at 7,000 BC while the earliest indicator of man's presence in Co. Mayo is a Bann flake (so named because thousands were recovered from along the valley of the river Bann), which was found in the Urlaur/Kilmovee area in 1991 (Byrne et al 1991). Many archaeologists believe that these flakes served as an all-purpose hunting and fishing knife and they are associated with the Later Mesolithic period 5,500-3,500 BC (Mallory and McNeill 1991, 24).

Brackloon Wood is a typical Atlantic oakwood of 74 hectares dominated by the sessile oak and located three miles SSW of Westport town on the foothills of Croagh Patrick. Physically the townland of Brackloon consists of a large (333 acres) undulating and hilly area bordered by the Owenwee River along the eastern flank and containing a former lake, Brackloon Lough, near the centre; this is now virtually reduced to a marshy pond due to ingrowth by wet woodland vegetation. The wood is owned and managed by Coillte and has been the focal point of various environmental projects over the past ten years or so. The oak forest was underplanted with conifers in the 1960s and it is a Coillte pilot forest for the new native woodland improvement scheme.

A programme of research commenced at the wood in January 1998; its aims were to identify distinctive stages in the vegetation development since the end of the last ice age, to evaluate the current status of the ecosystem of the wood and to assess the impact of human and other activity on this ecosystem. Woodlands such as that at Brackloon are dominated by organisms with very long life cycles, and ecological processes such as soil development and vegetation succession can take several hundred years to develop. Among the main aims of the study was to determine the role played by human activity in the evolution of the vegetation of Brackloon Wood (if any), and to assess the impact such human interference had on the ecology there. The following summary account of the palaeoecological study of Brackloon Wood is an edited version of the original copy kindly supplied by the authors pre-publication (Engelbrechten, McGee, Little and Mitchell).

14

Three sites in the wood were chosen, and both fossil pollen analysis (polynology) and radiometric dating of sediment sequences were used. The use of polynology indicates when certain species of tree entered the Brackloon landscape and also highlights changes to the environment brought about by human activity. All dates given are uncorrected radiocarbon years before present (BP) with 0 BP = AD 1950. Of the three sites selected the one just S of Brackloon Lough proved the oldest and most rewarding. It probably had a larger pollen source area in the past when it was a larger lake than it is today. In general, the larger the size of the basin from which the sediment is derived, the larger its pollen catchment or pollen source area will be (Jacobsen and Bradshaw 1981). Relatively speaking though, Brackloon Lough was a small catchment basin, and as a result, its preserved pollen is predominantly of local origin and ideal for tracing the history of this individual forest stand.

Nationally the period at the end of the last ice age saw a gradual increase in temperature with a corresponding spread in the growth of juniper and empetrum heath. The fossil pollen at Brackloon Lough shows the emergence of juniper at c. 10,710 BP. By about 10,370 BP, tall shrub and open woodland of birch and willow, rich in grasses and sedges, was flourishing. Further changes at c. 10,235 BP saw hazel gain a firm foothold, with birch and, to a lesser extent, willow, still present. The period from c. 8,705 to 6,350 BP saw the expansion of deciduous woodland with hazel, elm, oak and birch to the forefront. Bracken appeared in the pollen for the first time in c. 8,025 BP.

The continuation of this deciduous woodland is evident in the next phase c. 6,530 to 4,585 BP, which also witnessed a dramatic increase of alder, a wet-loving tree, at the start of this time period. A minor peak (0.7%) in the occurrence of plantain grass occurs at c. 5,580 BP and this could be significant in marking the arrival of the first colonisers to this place, and perhaps to the area in general. This date fits into Neolithic times, and monuments such as the rock art stone at Boheh (1) and some cairns on Croagh Patrick (21) and (23) may be the creation of their not-too-distant descendants.

A pre-bog field system in Owenwee with associated circular enclosure (Fig. 9) could possibly date from around this time. We may never know if the initial attempt at tree felling in the Brackloon Wood of Neolithic times was the work of a few solitary individuals, or a larger scale co-operative effort; in nearby Owenwee, however, the field system is indicative of community fencing, similar but on a much smaller scale to that uncovered at the Céide Fields in North Mayo.

At the start of the next phase c. 4,585 to 2,065 BP, open woodland was still prevalent with fern and heather also present. Human interference is suggested by the decline of elm (ulmus) at c. 3,205 BP, oak at c. 2,845 BP and alder at c. 2,485 BP. The probable effect of increased human activity is suggested by a significant spike in the plantain pollen at about 1,200-1,000 BC, which fits securely into the Bronze Age and is possibly reflected archaeologically in the numerous fulacht fiadha from the general locality. It was during this period that the vegetation in the Brackloon Lough area was at its most diverse both structurally and in terms of variety, and this diversity was maintained by constant disturbance here. A large-scale build-up of sediment caused a gradual shallowing of the lake basin at Brackloon Lough.

There is a noticeable lull in the occurrence of plantain grass from about 2,300 BP to 1,800 BP which corresponds with the Iron Age in Ireland, and these findings are replicated in numerous similar surveys from around the country. This lull can be interpreted as a drop in population during this period or some similar factor, which led to a partial regeneration of local woodlands; at Brackloon Lough, hazel and alder pollen show a surge during the corresponding years.

From the third to fourth centuries AD, to the start of the eighth century, an even greater peak in the grass pollen becomes evident. Also dating from this period are the raths, cashels and ringforts (see below), where individual family units dwelt at that time. A homestead was established in a cashel (148) only 300m to the SSE of Brackloon Lough on slightly raised ground. That these farmers were more concerned with animal husbandry and the rearing of animals is suggested from the lack of cereal pollen in the analysis. To facilitate more efficient farming practice in an ever-increasing population tree clearing operations must have been the norm at this time.

The final section from the vertical core of sediment dates from c. 710 AD up to the present time (1998). This saw the introduction of beech and a partial recovery of the local woodland. Samples of charcoal spreads and pits in the wood have been dated to the sixteenth and seventeenth centuries, with the charcoal, doubtless used as fuel for a furnace in the locality. There was an old iron mill shown in nearby Knappaghmore (O.S. 88, 053) on the 1838 O.S. map, which would have required charcoal. The accumulation of nutrients and sediment at Brackloon Lough resulted in its conversion to a willow swamp from about 1,600 AD, and its upper 0.85m today is composed of peat. Whereas the core from Brackloon Lough went to a depth of 12.16m, that from the second test core near the Owenwee River only achieved 1.2m in depth. At the latter, the pollen samples dating from 5,075 ± 75 BP have general similarities with those from Brackloon Lough.

Conclusion

Though the main test site at Brackloon Lough is rather small in area, the pollen analysis represents local vegetation changes and also shows evidence for human impact. The increase in plantain grass at 5580 BC, which heralds the first attempt at a partial woodland clearance, fits comfortably into the Later Mesolithic. No Mesolithic occupation sites have as yet been detected in Mayo and a look at the distribution map of Early Mesolithic sites from Ireland shows most located in low-lying areas and near rivers, lakes or the sea shore (Mallory and McNeill 1991, 16) – similar to that along the S shore of Clew Bay. The domination of the natural woodland over several thousand years is more reflective of small population numbers and emphasises the inability of Mesolithic, Neolithic or Bronze Age man to make noticeable inroads on the forests. Only with the increase in population during the Early Christian period did communities finally succeed in clearing the woodland; so much so in fact that man was able to erect a homely cashel where his livestock could graze freely in this presumably large, cleared area. However, nature wins through in the end and freed from the chains of man, the current wood has regenerated itself.

Trees and shrubs which registered in the pollen analysis but no longer survive here include pine, yew, juniper, alder and poplar, while more recent arrivals include rhododendron and spruce.

Chapter 3

Croagh Patrick Summit

3.1 Introduction

A twentieth-century church crowns the summit of Croagh Patrick. Its erection dates back to 1905 with additional wings added on in 1962. Before the 1994-5 excavations were begun, a full documentary and aerial survey of the mountain top was carried out.

Evidence for an early church or churches is available in references to claims for church taxes from buildings on the summit in 824 and 1216 AD. In 1838, O'Donovan stated that pilgrims entered the little chapel of Teampall Phádraig, knelt at the altar and recited prayers. He also held that the rude little chapel built by St. Patrick was this Teampall Phádraig. He described a building 16 feet long whose east gable was 8 feet high and inside of which stood a stone altar. While 8 feet wide at the east end, the building was only 5 feet wide at the entrance (presumably at the west end). He also mentioned that the church was surrounded by an irregular circle of stones.

Plate 1: Cave-like church on summit in 1904.

In 1904 an article in the London Daily Chronicle entitled *An Irish Pilgrimage* stated that the church built by St. Patrick was located in a hollow-like crater close to the summit, which had lately been roofed by corrugated iron sheets weighted down by piles of rock (see plate 1). Nearly all available maps of the mountain indicate a church on its summit. A matter of significance during the course of the 1904 church construction was that workers came upon human remains in the foundations. While these could be evidence of an early ecclesiastical burial ground on the site at that time, they speculated that the remains were those of Robert Binn or 'Bob of the Reek', a local man who lived on the summit for fourteen years early in the nineteenth century. As a way of life, he did penance or pilgrimage to the summit for those who were unable to do so. During his life, he expressed a wish to be buried on the summit and his wish was granted following his death, and O.S. maps show his grave just south of Casán Phadraig near the summit.

The best description of the mountain rampart wall comes from Ottway in 1839 when he described a low wall of large stones, evidently of the most ancient construction (see p. 82). O'Donovan mentions a path which ran around the circular verge of the apex of the mountain. Some of the group photographs from Harry Hughes publication show pilgrims standing on broad, built-up ground on the summit, which may be interpreted as substantial remains of the enclosing rampart wall, early in the twentieth century (1973; 15, 21, 26, 27).

A 1973 aerial photograph of the mountain top (p. 25) is a valuable aid in the identification of features visible then, where all the main elements on the mountain show up quite clearly. Along with the 1905 church, the outline of the rampart wall appears almost in its entirety, with religious stalls superimposed on or into it. The areas named on O.S. maps as Leaba Phádraig and Teampall Phádraig show up clearly as well defined circular and nearly rectangular outlines respectively. Finally, several of the hut sites or hut hollows on the outer upper edge of the mountain are also easily identified from this image.

3.2 Excavations on the Summit

The first phase of archaeological excavations on the summit of the mountain was carried out in August and September 1994. One specific area roughly 25m to the E of St. Patrick's Oratory (built in 1905) was selected, this being the approximate location where Teampall Phádraig was shown on earlier O.S. maps. In the early stages, the remains of makeshift stone structures, possibly religious stalls, were uncovered.

Oratory (Plates 16a, 16b)

Close by lay the remains of a rectangular building which measured 5.52m N-S by 7.76m E-W overall, and 3.5m N-S by 5.57m E-W internally. Its surviving remains showed a dry-stone building using flat schist flags forming a rather smooth wall face, especially in the interior. The construction flag stones used in the walls averaged 0.04m long and 0.03m wide. Corbelling, whereby overlapping stones brought the building to a narrow top, was in use here, as evidenced at the S and E walls. Excavation also revealed that the S wall and SW corner were cut into the natural rock. No clear outer wall face on the S side could be determined, while inner facing varied from 0.2m high along N wall to reach 1.16m high along W wall.

Entrance

An E-W alignment with the doorway facing west is an almost ubiquitous Early Christian church layout. Here however, and probably on account of its lofty exposed location, the doorway was facing E. The two sides of the opening were 0.68m apart, better preserved on the southern side and inclined slightly off vertical. Its entrance was graced by a flat threshold stone 1.2m long and 0.7m wide, with rudimentary sockets on either side of the doorway, within the church. These sockets took the form of twin post holes on the northern side, indicating the use of double posts here; both post holes were rectangular in plan and overall they measured 0.3m deep, 0.42m N-S and 0.28m E-W while they contained an iron nail, another small iron object and a further small iron fragment. The post hole on S side of door was U-shaped in profile, measuring 0.3m N-S by 0.2m E-W and 0.32m deep. Its use as an anchor post for a door is indicated by the curved wear to the side of one of its component stones.

Stratigraphy

The final phase of the excavation showed bare rock forming the bedrock, with occasional narrow spreads of gravel just above this. This gravel layer extended under the eastern half of the N wall of the oratory in what was seen by the director as an attempt to level out the ground here prior to construction. Two organic layers both 0.08m thick were revealed above the gravel, with the upper of the two formed of peat and found to contain three flints, an animal bone, one fragment of iron and one possibly worked stone. Directly above this, a mainly dark soil layer was intermingled with flagstones and smaller chipped stones; parts of this layer may have formed the original flooring for the church; items recovered included three shards of native medieval pottery (thirteenth to fifteenth century), two heavily corroded bronze pins, two worked pieces of flint, and further possibly worked stones along with small fragments of iron. Artefacts from more recent times, including a 1971 German coin and some modern glass, had worked their way down to this level also; and near the centre of the oratory, an area of charcoal lay on either side of a line of set flagstones. This charcoal spread reached up to 0.34m thick and covered an area 1.7m N-S by 3.3m E-W while some iron fragments were recovered from its lower levels. This area was overlain by large flat flags from 0.22m to 0.52m in thickness, providing evidence that the structure had at least partially collapsed inwards. Among the rubble, some modern glass and iron fragments were uncovered. The upper layer of the excavation showed the side walls and oratory interior covered by a narrow band 0.2m thick (at most) of topsoil and stones which produced modern coins and religious medals.

Summary

A sample of charcoal from the excavation was sent for analysis and provided a radiocarbon date of 430 to 890 AD. Dry stone corbelled oratories such as this one are among the earliest of the Irish stone churches. They have their origins in earlier wooden oratories while their construction without the use of mortar is equally as ingenious, though on a smaller scale, as that applied at passage graves like Newgrange. Gallarus Oratory on the Dingle peninsula is Ireland's most complete Early Christian corbelled oratory. The post holes which were revealed at ground level inside the door of the oratory were probably accompanied higher up on the wall by matching recessed stones similar to hanging eyes, and through which the upper parts of the posts were inserted for retention. Finally, these remains are unlikely to be those located on the summit by O'Donovan (1838) and which he referred to as Teampall Phádraig. The chapel he described then is not dissimilar in length from this one. His width, however, is given as between 1.52m and 2.44m. It is likely that Croagh Patrick contained a number of successive churches and other buildings on its summit.

* * *

In 1995, six further cuttings were excavated on the mountain top (Fig. 2). Four of these were laid out across the 'rampart' wall, this being the name applied to the wall enclosing the summit of Croagh Patrick, while two cuttings embraced two of the twenty or so huts near the summit.

Cutting I

Located some 20m to WNW of the 1905 church. Across the rampart wall, this L-shaped trench measured 15.2m N-S by 6.7m E-W. Only the inner face of the rampart wall survived, rather poorly preserved and reaching a maximum height of 0.6m. Stones used in its construction were of schist and generally flat, between 0.6m and 0.8m in length, from 0.3m to 0.5m in width and averaged 0.1m thick. There was no outer facing to the rampart wall, rather this area was occupied by a mass of loose stones to a considerable depth; the same applied at cuttings III, IV and V.

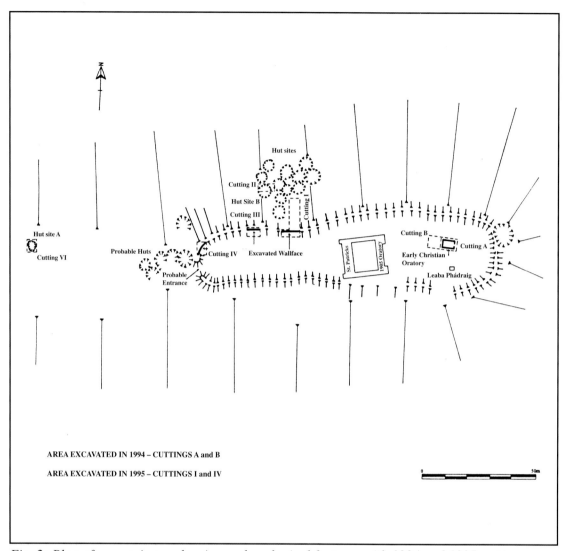

Fig. 2: Plan of mountain top showing archaeological features with 1994 and 1995 cuttings.

Stratigraphy

In general the stratigraphy here was very shallow. However, just inside and against the rampart wall it reached its greatest height at 0.2m. Here, a possible layer of rough paving overlay the natural bedrock and scree. A possible chert core fragment was recovered from this paved area. Just above this layer was a grey sandy silty context 0.05m thick which contained one blue glass bead (no. 3), two iron fragments and two flint chips. A thin layer of stone, rubble and soil 0.1m thick containing a broken and burnt chert flake lay above this, while the modern sod cover formed the upper level here.

Cutting II

Located 13m NW of Cutting I. This cutting was rectangular in plan, 3m N-S by 8m E-W, and cut across the northern half of a small hut (Hut B). Overall diameters for this circular hut measured 5m while its collapsed enclosing wall survived only to a height of 0.2m. Naturally occurring rock outcrop and scree formed the bedrock material within the hut. Above this lay a band of peat 0.15m thick, which had a spread of charcoal through it. From among the charcoal a broken chert flake fragment and a minute bronze fragment along with a modern penny were found.

Cutting III

Located 10m to W of Cutting I, it measured 3m N-S by 6m E-W and contained a 0.5m high section of the rampart wall inner face. Stratigraphy was very shallow and it contained no features or artefacts.

Cuttings IV and V

These initially were positioned inside and outside the rampart wall, but eventually merged to form a trench 6m N-S by 4m E-W. Relating to artefacts, this was the most productive of all cuttings, though not all were from secure archaeological contexts. A further stretch of the mountain top rampart wall inner face survived here to 0.5m in height.

Stratigraphy

As elsewhere, it was generally shallow, though up to 0.3m deep just inside the rampart wall. Here, the base of the cutting was formed of loose scree with a grey sandy layer containing small rounded pebbles above this. One yellow glass bead (no. 1), a possible sharpening stone and a broken retouched flint flake came from this sandy context. In the area between this layer and the topsoil, a white glass bead (no. 8), a small chert flake and an incomplete metal mount were retrieved. The topsoil was of a peaty nature averaging 0.1m thick and it produced three blue glass beads (nos. 5, 9 and 11), two black glass beads (no. 2), two amber beads (nos. 6 and 7) and one purple glass bead (no. 10). Along with these, one broken retouched flint flake was found. Another black glass bead (no. 4) was recovered from the sod beneath the upper rampart wall collapse.

Cutting VI

Located 75m to the W of the rampart wall at the last cutting. It measured 6m N-S and E-W and it contained a small oval hut 3.2m N-S by 1.7m E-W (Hut A). The collapsed wall of the hut varied from 0.45m thick on E side to 1m thick along W, while it averaged 0.3m high. No stone facing was in evidence. Bedrock was overlain by a peaty layer of 0.14m thick which contained a broken retouched flint flake, a small chert flake and a chert chip. Topsoil only 0.1m thick above this was formed of a sod/peat mix.

* * *

The occurrence of so many beads from the excavation (p. 22) proved of immense interest. All were from a single glass colour of either black, blue, white, purple or yellow. However, none proved reliable as regards dating, in relation to their shape or composition, or as regards their find contexts. The two amber beads, which could indicate a Late Bronze Age presence, cannot be relied on for dating purposes, as both came from an upper sod layer. Blue glass beads appear to date anywhere from the Iron Age to the early Medieval period. Three of these (nos. 5, 9 and 11) are of a deep blue colour and Warner (1981, 60) contends that this deep blue glass, as a general rule of thumb, belongs between the third century BC and the fourth century AD. Small blue glass beads similar to no. 11 were obtained from Iron Age contexts in excavations at Knowth, Co. Meath (Egan 1974) and at Grannagh, Co. Galway (Raftery 1981). Glass beads of a yellow colour have been obtained at several Early Christian sites, though the segmentation to the example here (no. 1) is rare.

The Glass Beads (Plate 26)

- No. 1: Yellow glass bead with one half missing. It is B-shaped in cross section. Estimated overall diameter 12.5mm, estimated width of central perforation 6.5mm and thickness 6.3mm; from Cutting IV.
- No. 2: Complete spherical black glass bead, with striations on the surface. Overall diameter 10.3mm, central perforation is 3.2mm across and the bead is 8.9mm thick; from Cutting IV.
- No. 3: Half a blue glass spherical bead. Estimated overall diameter 10.1mm, estimated width of central perforation 4.7mm and thickness 8.3mm; from Cutting I.
- No. 4: A complete spherical opaque black glass bead bearing extremely fine striations. Overall diameter 10.9mm, central perforation is 3.4mm across and it is 9.1mm thick. This was the heaviest of all beads at 1.6g; from Cutting IV.
- No. 5: Half a deep blue glass bead, oval in shape and slightly flattened at the top and base. Estimated overall diameter 11mm, central perforation is 3.4mm across and it is 7.4mm thick; from Cutting IV.
- No. 6: One half of a spherical amber bead with flattened parallel sides. Estimated overall diameter 15mm, estimated width of central perforation 2.5mm and thickness 10.3mm; from Cutting IV.
- No. 7: One half of a spherical amber bead with flattened sides. Estimated overall diameter 15mm, estimated width of central perforation 6.3mm and thickness 11.2mm; from Cutting IV.
- No. 8: Non-symmetrical, cylindrical-shaped white opaque glass bead. Maximum overall diameter is 6.7mm and central perforation, which is off-centre, is 2.1mm across at most. The bead is 5.6mm thick; from cutting IV.
- No. 9: A lop-sided oval-shaped deep blue glass bead. Maximum overall diameter 5.5mm, central perforation 2.2mm and thickness 4mm; from Cutting IV.
- No. 10: Roughly cylindrical-shaped deep purple glass bead. Maximum diameter 5.7mm, central perforation 2.3mm and it is 4mm thick; from Cutting IV.
- No. 11: Cylindrical blue glass bead 5.7mm across at most, central perforation 2.2mm across and 4mm thick at most; from Cutting IV.
- No. 12: Spherical black glass bead with striations on the surface. Maximum diameter of 8.5mm, with central perforation 4mm wide, it is 8.7mm thick at most; from Cutting IV.

Lithics

The lithics assemblage consists almost exclusively of chert or flint and was recovered from both the rampart wall area and the interior of Hut B. However, the broken chert flake fragment from the latter was extremely small and unhelpful to any analysis. Elsewhere, the lithics took the form of flakes and core fragments or chips, while a broken re-touched flint flake from Hut A could be an indicator of early settlement.

3.3 Historical References

While the majority of the material contained in this book is of an archaeological nature, mention must also be given to historical references to Croagh Patrick. Evidence of prehistoric activity of possibly ritual significance is to be found locally at the rock art of Boheh (1), at the cairns near the summit (21, 23) and at the collection of ancient monuments on the seashore at Gortbraud, Killadangan (37, 38, 83, 129 and 231). The well known pilgrimage of modern and medieval times has in all likelihood endured since Early Christian times and may even have its roots in earlier prehistoric ritual here.

The difficulties in tracing the history of Saint Patrick and his direct impact on Ireland and her people, are best described by Ó Corráin (Foster [ed.] 1989, 9,10):

> Ireland is indebted overwhelmingly to Britain for its Christianity, and the most famous of British missionaries is Saint Patrick. He is generally regarded as the greatest of Ireland's missionaries, but his history presents difficulties at every turn. He left behind two works, his *Confession* and his *Letter to the soldiers of Coroticus*. The first is spiritual biography and justification of his mission, the second a letter of protest against the enslavement of some of his new Irish converts. Neither is intended to provide a life-story or a history of the conversion. We know only a few facts about him and these do not include the date of his birth, that of his mission to Ireland, or that of his death, though it seems reasonable to place his mission in the first half and middle of the fifth century. He was born in western Britain and was the son of a deacon and minor official who had a country estate; he was captured at the age of 16 by Irish raiders and shipped as a slave to Ireland, where he remained, probably in north Connacht, for six years; he escaped, travelled 200 miles, and shipped out of Ireland with a pagan crew; the Irish continued to haunt his thoughts, and he returned to them (perhaps as a bishop, though probably not part of any official mission) to preach the gospel; he worked hard, experienced danger and hardship, and suffered the bitter criticism of his own countrymen, who questioned his fitness for his mission; he won many converts and penetrated into parts of the country where no Christian missionary had gone before; and he asserted, with some considerable emphasis, that he was a bishop. So much is clear from his own writings. All the rest is uncertain, at best. It seems likely that Patrick's memory was cherished in the north-east, particularly in Armagh and its neighbourhood. The expansion of his cult (a carefully crafted undertaking of the clergy of Armagh) took place later when Armagh claimed apostolic precedence and primacy, and it had spread widely, even into Munster, by the late seventh century.

Ó Corráin continues with a brief account of early monastic Ireland (ibid, 10):

> Monasticism (and monastic ideas are very much present in St. Patrick's writings) made rapid strides in the Irish church of the sixth century, but the great monasteries which sprang up in this period do not claim Patrick or his disciples as their founders. Originally retreats from the world, places of asceticism, and stricter discipline, the monasteries soon attracted the patronage of the rich and powerful, and themselves became influential institutions on many levels. These great self-governing monastic churches, each with its own rule, its own organization, and its own estates, became in time the bearers of a rich and varied literary and artistic culture, and provided the patronage and the economic support necessary for the cultivation of high art.

The simplistic notion that Patrick applied this new religion across the land in one lightning strike, is warned against when Ó Corráin adds (ibid, 8):

> The conversion of the whole of Ireland was a much slower and more complex business. The concentration of historians on the life and writings of Saint Patrick – not to mention the successful cultivation of his legend from the seventh century, and the central place it has won for itself in the Irish consciousness through the centuries – has tended to distort the story of the conversion and draw away attention from the other missionaries. Yet, in the seventh-century dossier of Patrick, some evidence of other missionaries is preserved, though these are represented as submitting to the claims of Patrick.

Two notable works deal with much of Saint Patrick's life and missionary work; *The Confessions of Saint Patrick* was apparently written in his august years while *The Tripartite Life of Saint Patrick* was written in Irish in or about the tenth century.

Oral tradition and one local place name (Lugnademon) maintain that snakes were driven from Ireland during Patrick's time on the mountain, though more likely this may have been a metaphor for the banishment of our old pagan ways and customs. In *The Tripartite Life*, one reference states that no demons came to this land following Patrick's vigil on Croagh Patrick. If the snakes or demons symbolise paganism then Croagh Patrick and its summit must have represented one of the foremost sacred ritual places in all of Ireland.

Some of the earliest references to the mountain refer to Croagh Patrick as Mons Egli, Croachan Aigli or Cruachan Aigli. It is not known when exactly his Christian name was incorporated into the mountain but according to *The Annals of Connaught*, the peak was known as Cruaich Patric by 1351. Only with the widespread anglicisation of so many Irish place names in the sixteenth century did it thus become known as Croagh Patrick.

The archaeological excavations of 1994 uncovered the walls and collapsed roof of a simple oratory. Whether or not this was the same Teampall Phádraig which was at the centre of a dispute between the archbishops of Armagh and Tuam in 824 AD cannot be stated with certainty. The dispute arose over Armagh's request for church income from St. Patrick's Oratory on the mountain top and Tuam's refusal of this request (Hughes 1991, 20). In 1216, the Archbishop of Tuam appealed successfully to Rome to rescind the payment of this tax to Armagh, especially as the chapel had been built by the Archbishop of Tuam (ibid.). Successive churches have probably crowned some part of the summit over various periods, while a focal point of today's stations, namely a hollow called Leaba Phádraig, may have incorporated part of an early oratory originally. The present church on the summit was erected in 1905 with renovations carried out in the early 1960s. Prior to this, a temporary make-shift church had been erected in 1883 and this survived until August 14, 1904 when mass was celebrated at it for the last time (ibid.).

Pilgrimage has taken place here on several different dates over the best part of two millennia. St. Patrick's Day March 17th has featured prominently as the official pilgrimage day though inclement weather no doubt forced a move away from that date. According to *The Annals of Ulster*, lightning killed thirty of those fasting on the mountain in 1113 AD during a March pilgrimage.

The commonest dates for this annual event are and have been the last Friday of July (Garland Friday) and the last Sunday of July. These connect it with the ancient Celtic festival of Lughnasa (August 1st) which celebrated and marked the start of the harvest season. A possible connection with harvesting and planting has also been suggested as an explanation for the decoration on the rock outcrop at Boheh (p. 28, 29). The last Sunday of July, or Reek Sunday as it is referred to locally, is also known as Domhnach Chrom Dubh – Crom Dubh was traditionally a pagan god who lived on or near Croagh Patrick (Hughes 1991, 86). A third date sometimes used for pilgrimage is the Feast of the Assumption on August 15th. This feast day is known in Irish as 'Lá Fhéile Mhuire Mór sa bFhómhar', or the great feast of Mary of the harvest (ibid.). One of the stations of the mountain pilgrimage is called Roilig Mhuire and perhaps the group of cairns at these stations and the August 15th date predate any ecclesiastical activity on Croagh Patrick.

* * *

References to Local Buildings and Artefacts

Later church history tells us that the first order to be established in Co. Mayo was by the Franciscans at Straide between 1240 and 1250 (O'Hara 1982, 16). Some two centuries later, the only Gaelic foundation of the period was established at Murrisk. This was a house of Augustinian hermits similar to those in Ballinrobe, Ballyhaunis, Burriscarra and Dunmore.

The only other historic building to receive a mention was Belclare Castle (263) which unfortunately no longer survives. References to it are scant and generally uninformative, telling us little more than that it was an O'Malley stronghold on the shores of Clew Bay three miles SW of Westport House (Knox 1908, 305).

Some notable artefacts worthy of mention are the Black Bell of St. Patrick (Clog Dubh) and some chalices from Murrisk Friary. The former is a bronze coated iron object with a manufacture date of between 600 and 900 AD (Hughes 1991, 56, following a study of Irish Bells by Cormac Bourke of the Ulster Museum). At least three chalices have been manufactured which relate directly to Murrisk Friary or one of its brethren (ibid.). One of these, dated 1724, is now under the care of the Church of Ireland clergy in Westport.

* * *

Gold

References to gold from early historic times are as scarce as gold dust itself. One tentative translation and account of *The Tripartite Life of St. Patrick* by Whitley Stokes in 1887 states '*of the idols worshipped in pagan Ireland, one named Cromm Cruaich is said to have been specially venerated, as it was made of gold*'. It is said to have been the chief idol of Ireland and also a special god of Foilges (ibid.). Apart from references, the original Irish translation of the Owenwee (buí = yellow or gold) River, which rises on the mountain is a strong indicator of gold being present and recognised along its course from earlier times. It is well recognised now that traces of gold do turn up in several of West Mayo's mountain streams – particularly those running off Croagh Patrick, along with other hills and mountains to the west and south west. A place near the northern edge of Pollanoughty townland was given the name 'lug-an-óir' or the 'hollow of gold' by O'Donovan in 1838.

Plate 2: View of mountain top features in 1973.

Chapter 4

Catalogue of Sites

Introduction

All site numbers used in the catalogue have been adapted for use by the R.M.P. (Record of Monuments and Places, formerly the S.M.R.) office in Dublin. Where a monument has been shown on any earlier O.S. map, it is represented on the listing by a sign marked ✔. Along with 6″ O.S. map numbers, other information with each site type includes townland name, plan and trace, co-ordinates and metric height above sea level. Use the example of the first site in the catalogue (p. 28) as a signpost to the information available in formal layout for each monument type.

1 – Each site on the survey has its own specific reference number and this relates solely to the Croagh Patrick Archaeological Survey. Hence the first site is number **1**.

Boheh (E.D. Knappagh) – This refers to the townland name, which in this case is Boheh. However there are two townlands from the survey named Boheh and to differentiate between them, the Electoral Division they belong to is enclosed in brackets; hence this monument is located in Boheh townland, in the Electoral Division of Knappagh. The other townland of Boheh is better known locally as Bouris and within this catalogue it is found as Boheh (in the Electoral Division of Kilsallagh).

O.S. 97 indicates that the monument and/or its location is to be found on the 6″ Ordnance Survey map number 97 for Co. Mayo. There are 123 6″ O.S. maps for the entire county of Mayo.

O.S. 97:4:6 – The numbers 4 (plan) and 6 (trace) give the general position of the monument on the map, by breaking the map up into a series of squares (see Fig. 2).

(9130 5163) are the metric co-ordinates and are measured off the 6″ O.S. map. Hence the site in Boheh (E.D. Knappagh) is 91.3cms from the left margin of the map (Easting) and 51.63cms from the bottom margin of the map (Northing).

S.M.R. 006 shows it is site number 6 on its map. Most site numbers were allocated to the monuments by the Sites and Monuments Record Office in Dublin in 1991. Any new sites locally continue numerically from where the S.M.R. left off.

The *OD* or Ordnance Datum is the height above sea level at which the monument is located on a metric scale, and the Boheh monument is situated between sixty-one and ninety-one metres above sea level.

St. Patrick's Chair indicates the name that was attached to this site on one or more of the earlier 6″ O.S. maps and shows the form of writing that the name took.

In relation to the sites, many of them were represented on earlier 6″ O.S. maps dating from 1838 to 1844 and various years early in the twentieth century (depending on the map). The Survey required the use of all or part of six 6″ O.S. maps, namely numbers 86, 87, 88, 96, 97 and 98. Not surprisingly, forts (including raths, cashels and unspecific enclosures) are the most numerously represented antiquities on the six inch maps; of a total of ninety-four such monuments, thirty-one had never been represented on any earlier O.S. map (or any other known map for that matter). While prominent buildings like Murrisk Friary and the former castle at Belclare were clearly represented, such is not the case with other less pronounced monuments. All the early ecclesiastical sites were shown on earlier maps, while on the other hand, of the fifty or so hut sites described, only four had ever previously been represented cartographically. None of the twenty-seven fulacht fiadha from the list ever featured as monuments or places of interest, as early mappers together with early antiquarians were not as aware of these sites compared, for example, with cashels or standing stones.

Many of the newly detected sites were discovered initially by members of the survey team; however, a considerable number also came to light due to conversations with landowners and other interested locals.

It should be noted that the inclusion of any or all sites in the catalogue below is not an invitation for people to randomly decide to visit these monuments without prior notification to the landowner in question.

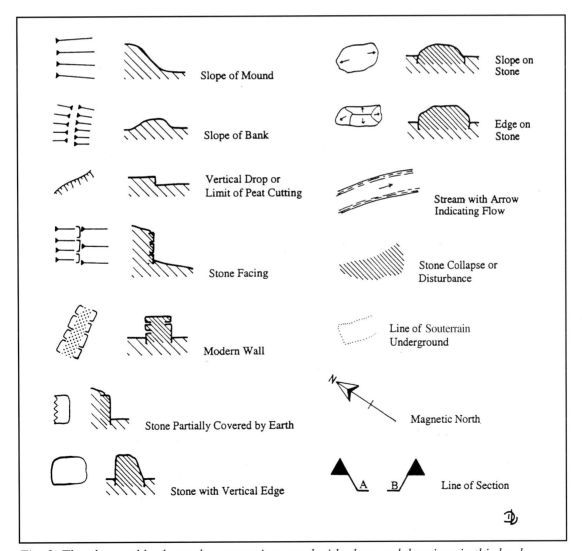

Fig. 3: The above table shows the conventions used with plans and drawings in this book.

ROCK ART 1

The record of the monuments starts with one unique example of rock art, which possibly spans the Neolithic and Early Bronze Age periods (Bradley, 1997). Its location in clear sight of Croagh Patrick and a large area of low-lying ground to the W gives the site considerable views over an extensive landscape.

Attempting to determine the significance or meaning of rock art has proven rather difficult. However, two general schools of thought are held. Firstly, that it is the art, decoration or carving itself that is important, and an ability to decipher it would provide a better understanding of the people who carved them (van Hoek in *Cathair na Mart* 1995, 15-19).

Secondly, that it is the location, and not strictly the carvings that should be examined to help unravel the mystery behind rock art (Bracken and Wayman in *Cathair na Mart* 1992, 1-11). Our earliest hunter-gatherer ancestors must surely have practised a system of land tenure, based primarily on paths and vantage points (Bradley 1997); it appears likely that both prehistoric and Early Christian paths to Croagh Patrick passed immediately beside the local rock art stone at Boheh.

Additionally, there is the possible argument that it was early prospectors for metals and gold who created the carvings, as a signpost that the minerals they so desperately sought were indeed available in this locality (Morris 1979, 16-17). There is also the phenomenon of the 'Rolling Sun' on the sides of Croagh Patrick, as viewed from the rock art stone at Boheh (Bracken and Wayman 1992, 5-11) treated of on the next page.

There is one further known example of rock art from County Mayo in Cooslughoga, SW of Ballinrobe (O.S. 120, 05103). Over half the distribution of Irish rock art sites comes from counties Donegal and Kerry. Another concentration near Dundalk is overlooked by the highest passage grave in Ireland at Slieve Gullion (Bradley 1997, 43). The occurrence of this passage grave on the upper slopes of a shallow valley leading down to an estuary (ibid., 43) can be compared with Boheh. Similar rock art sites in England are situated either directly above the entrances to the lower ground, or commanding views along the valley routes (ibid., 44) as at Boheh.

1 Boheh (E.D. Knappagh)
O.S. 97:4:6 (9130 5163)
Site 006 ✔ OD 61-91
St. Patrick's Chair
Plate 15a
Generally accepted as one of the best decorated rock art stones in Ireland and Britain, it is inscribed on a large sheet of natural rock outcrop 2m to 2.5m high. A large irregular segment on top has broken free from the main block, but this could even have happened prior to carving. The current extent of the outcrop measures 5.2m N-S by 4.8m E-W. Decoration is to be found on all surfaces at different levels and mainly takes the form of 'cup and ring' motifs. Most of the rings are circular while a considerable number touch, overlap or spring from each other. Other decorations include 'keyhole' and cross motifs, with an inscribed cross on the N side possibly associated with Penal times.

ROLLING SUN SPECTACLE

This wonderfully decorated stone has been the focus of much study, speculation and debate over the past ten years or so. In the early 1990s, it was observed that the setting sun traced the silhouette of the north face of the mountain ridge of Croagh Patrick on two dates in the year (Bracken and Wayman 1992, 1-11). These two dates together with the Winter Solstice divide the year into three nearly equal parts which the authors felt could be significant in the sowing and harvest cycle of contemporary civilisations. On two specific dates in the year the setting sun, when viewed from here, was seen to line up with the northern slope of the mountain and then to gradually follow the slope as it descended (ibid., 6). In simplified terms, the spectacle would have resembled a golden disc rolling down one side of a perfect triangle before disappearing into darkness. Undoubtedly this phenomenon was observed by prehistoric peoples here, but the significance they attached to it may never be fully understood. Dates for this solar event, which was first observed and noted by Gerry Bracken of Westport, are April 18 and August 24 and these are seen as the respective annual dates for the planting and harvesting of the crops (ibid., 9). This theory connecting the Boheh stone with crop production certainly appears most plausible but more striking still is the pagan triangle formed by the mountain top, the midday sun and this mass of rock which became so decorated.

Plate 3: The rolling sun phenomenon as viewed from the Boheh stone.

SHELL MIDDENS 2-5

As the name suggests, these are made up of the discarded shells of edible molluscs which are normally found along the sea shore. Excavated examples from around Ireland indicate that they can date from the Mesolithic to relatively modern times. The presence of charcoal at many can serve as a good dating agent, and it may be evidence that the molluscs were cooked before consumption. Most consist of a rather thick build-up of sea shells and can extend in size from only a few metres up to 60m in length. Along the sea shore, several have undoubtedly been washed away by wave and tide action, though newly detected shell middens can also be uncovered by the same forces of nature; such was the case with the best preserved local example in Murrisknaboll (4). Not all are to be found by the sea, and two other examples were located 300m to 400m inland on higher ground. One of these (3) no longer survives, but luckily it was sampled by John Jackson, a geologist, during the course of a field trip. His notes together with those of the late Frank Mitchell are the only account now available of the site (Mitchell 1990, 125-6). Recent work from Connemara (J.R.S.A.I., 1998) has produced a range of dates for shell middens, ranging from the Early Bronze Age to the medieval period.

2 Killadangan
O.S. 87:12:1 (6935 2415)
Site 03502 OD 0-30
Large amounts of sea shells are incorporated into a bank at the base of the cashel wall (171) in its S sector. Some shells have been crushed, others are complete and include oysters and winkles. The midden had obviously been created prior to the construction of the cashel.

3 Killadangan
O.S. 87:12:1 (7285 2323)
Site 03702 OD 0-30
Nothing survives of this midden or of the enclosure (232) beside which it was located. Frank Mitchell on a visit here in 1983 recorded cockle, limpet, mussel, oyster and periwinkle shells together with pig and calf bones. Some shells were sent for analysis to Helsinki and were dated to approximately 1100 AD.

4 Murrisknaboll
O.S. 87:7:4 (5044 3182)
Site 077 OD 0-15
Plate 30b
Set into a low N facing cliff which rises 1.2m to 3.5m high. It stretches for 17m in length and averages 0.5m thick where best defined. Shells include scallops and winkles but mostly oyster, and stones are also found in the mix. Along W there is an exposed charcoal layer 0.45m thick. The slight promontory head here is called Clarebeg, and its coastal setting does not augur well for its long-term survival.

5 Rossbeg
O.S. 87:8:3 (8732 4115)
Site 075 OD 0-15
On an exposed clay/gravel shore face 1.3m high, it is formed primarily of a layer of charcoal from 0.04m to 0.07m thick. The topsoil above it is gravelly clay and varies from 0.36m to 0.42m thick. Beneath it is a harder, lighter coloured clay. Though no shells are visible at the site, its littoral location renders it most likely to be connected with the burning or cooking of some produce from the sea.

MEGALITHIC STRUCTURES 6-10

Among our earliest surviving monuments throughout Ireland are megalithic tombs or structures which date from the Neolithic / Early Bronze Age and served as our earliest known burial sites. They consist of stone-built burial chambers and most would originally have been contained in larger burial mounds or cairns. There are no definite megalithic tombs located within the survey area. However, two sites have been described whose component stones are of small dimensions typical of many of the tombs in the west of Ireland. While one (6) lies in isolation in an area of peat, the second (8) is located near the centre of a univallate earthen enclosure (235) in a more fertile area. A stone row in Killadangan (37), part of a large archaeological complex here, was named Cromlech on all earlier O.S. maps and further resembled a megalith by the rectangular representation of its plan on these maps (Fig. 4b). Megalithic tombs vary from simple wedge tombs and portal dolmens, to more elaborate court tombs and passage tombs. Kilgeever parish to the west of Croagh Patrick contains a fine example of a wedge tomb at Srahwee (locally referred to as altóir), and a court tomb in Lecarrow townland. Of the 108 or so known megalithic tombs from Mayo, 64 are known court tombs with most of these in the N half of the county; there are 19 wedge tombs while most of the remainder are unclassified (1999 R.M.P. update).

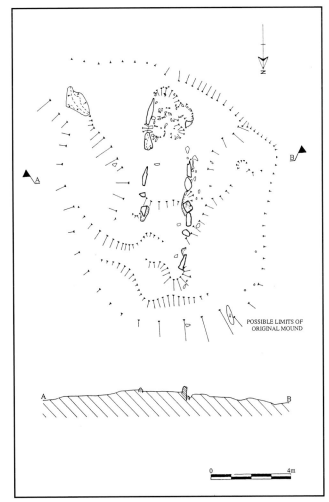

Fig. 4a: Possible megalithic gallery and retaining mound, Kilsallagh Lower (6).

Fig. 4b: Current stone alignment in Killadangan (37) was shown as a cromlech on 1840 map.

Extract from Ordnance Survey (1840)
© Government of Ireland Permit No. MP002001

31

6 Kilsallagh Lower
O.S. 86:16:3 (8785 1230)
Site 010 OD 91-122
Fig. 4a

In an area of heather-covered peat near the SW foot of Ben Goram, with excellent views from W to N over Clew Bay. This structure consists of a passage which is aligned NW-SE and is 8m long and 2.65m wide. It is composed of six low side stones on each side. The largest orthostat at SE measures 0.65m high, 1.3m long and 0.2m thick. At either end, the side stones curve slightly inwards. Its retaining mound, 0.5m high on average, measures 10m N-S by 12m E-W. The site is surrounded by numerous stone-built turf stacks, some of which may lie on earlier pre-bog walls. Superficially, this site appears to consist of the gallery of a megalithic tomb which is set in a substantial mound. However, the Megalithic Survey of Ireland urges a note of caution about it. The stones forming megalithic tombs are always firmly set into the ground and then surrounded or covered by a cairn or mound. At this site, the stones of the gallery-like feature, many of which have fallen, appear to be loosely set on the top of the mound.

7 Knockfin
O.S. 88:9:1 (0315 2955)
Site 08602 ✔ OD 30-61
Plate 13b

Located just to NE of the centre of a sub-circular univallate enclosure (235). This feature, from which the townland name is possibly derived, consists of a passage 6.2m long N-S and open at S end. The northern end stone 0.8m high is the tallest. Its western side is flanked by six low orthostats, while four line the E side and further low stones are also part of the feature. A low enclosing mound 0.2m to 0.4m high and 6m wide E-W survives at intervals between E and W. Again, the Megalithic Survey does not accept this site as a megalithic tomb. It suggests that the two rows of low upright stones form part of inner and outer facings of the S wall of a rectangular house site or small enclosure that measures about 8m by 8m.

Names which suggest the site of possible megalithic structures

Apart from the 'Cromlech' mentioned above (37), other terms applied to megalithic tombs include 'Leaba Diarmuid', 'Druids' Altars' or 'Giants' Graves'. In three of the townlands places were pointed out which the older local residents referred to as 'giants' graves'. While vague descriptions were given of stones that stood at some of these sites, it is not possible to state with certainty that they were part of a megalithic tomb or structure. Moreover, a pair of standing stones 14m apart in Fahburren (33) were also initially described to the survey as a 'giant's grave'.

8 Brackloon
O.S. 87:13:3 (8840 1215)
Site 109 OD 30-61

Locals referred to a large collection of rocks, 10m from the edge of the Owenwee River, as a 'giant's grave'. Field clearance in 1957 removed them.

9 Oughty
O.S. 97:11:5 (5925 0565)
Site 055 OD 122-152

The landowner recalled 'a collection of upright stones or pillars six feet high' which he cleared away in 1975. His father had called it a 'giant's grave'.

10 Letterbrock
O.S. 97:8:5 (8282 3390)
Site 032 OD 122-152

While no feature was ever recalled here, an area on top of a low drumlin was always referred to as 'The giant's grave' by the deceased former landowner and his father. Near the base of the same drumlin, a collection of large rough stones was checked for megalithic properties but they proved rather vague.

BURIAL MOUNDS, CAIRNS, BARROWS 11-26

Large burial mounds of earth or stone, or a combination of both, are thought to have their origin in the Late Neolithic/Early Bronze Age. Those of earth are referred to as tumuli, while those formed of stones are termed cairns. Within the scope of the survey, cairns are certainly the most impressive, with those at the base of the cone of Croagh Patrick of particular significance. Both groups (21 and 23) are associated with the modern pilgrimage on the mountain, but they were probably originally associated with a much earlier pagan ritual/worship. While one is situated on the edge of the ancient togher which ran westwards over much of the county, leading people to this sacred place, the second example lies on a continuation of this ancient trackway farther to the west. Because of its size and location, that at Sheean (22) is among the most impressive of all cairns in this vicinity; from it, there are extensive views over Clew Bay and the offshore islands to the west and over much of central Mayo to the east. While the cairn at Sheean is located some 3km outside of the survey area, it was felt necessary to include it as it is such a prominent monument and local landmark, and because of its dominant strategic location overlooking much of the county and most of our survey area. The most impressive and greatest concentration of cairns in County Mayo occur in the Ballinrobe area with those in Ballymacgibbon North, Knock North and Carn among the finest examples (Ballinrobe Survey, 1994).

Most of the mounds and tumuli recorded here are small and modest in appearance, yet they are undoubtedly man-made (apart perhaps from Sheeroe (17)). The newly detected group of six small mounds (11) beneath cut-away bog at Bellataleen may have formed a small cemetery and could provide western parallels for cemeteries at Carrowjames near Belcarra (Raftery 1939, 1940) and on Slieve Cairn hill, Treannagleeragh, outside Kiltimagh (Solan and Sublowski 1999, 317-18). The largest mound is at Thornhill (20) and is strikingly visible from S and W, though the view from it is none too commanding. The large mound at Leckanvey is included (17) here, for while it is obviously natural, it is also monumental in appearance and its name 'Sheeroe' reveals some significance attached to it locally. Many megalithic tombs are/were enclosed in mounds similar (though generally smaller) to this one, and perhaps the name of the site was partly in recognition of this fact.

Ring barrows can sometimes resemble ringforts in their general circular appearance, their siting and in their construction, and they are normally dated to the Iron Age. While there are various forms of barrow in Ireland, the ring barrow is the commonest and most distinctive type. A typical ring barrow consists of a central earthen mound, enclosed by a fosse or ditch, with a bank forming the outer ring to the site; their central mound can vary from 4m to 30m in overall diameter and these monuments were used almost exclusively for cremated burial.

We have three ring barrows located within the survey area. That in Letterbrock (24) is the most impressive, located on a drumlin, mostly surrounded by bog. Named 'Lissaphuca' locally and cartographically, it may subsequently have been used as a fort. Liscarney contains a ring barrow (25) high on a ridge with extensive views west over Croagh Patrick while some standing stones in the same field (now reduced to one) may have given the site further ritual significance. Unlike these two, the Moyhastin example (26) is low-lying, sheltered and unremarkable. An archaeological survey of Aghamore parish and its environs in east County Mayo recorded ten ring barrows, half of which were unmarked on any O.S. maps (1991 Byrne et al).

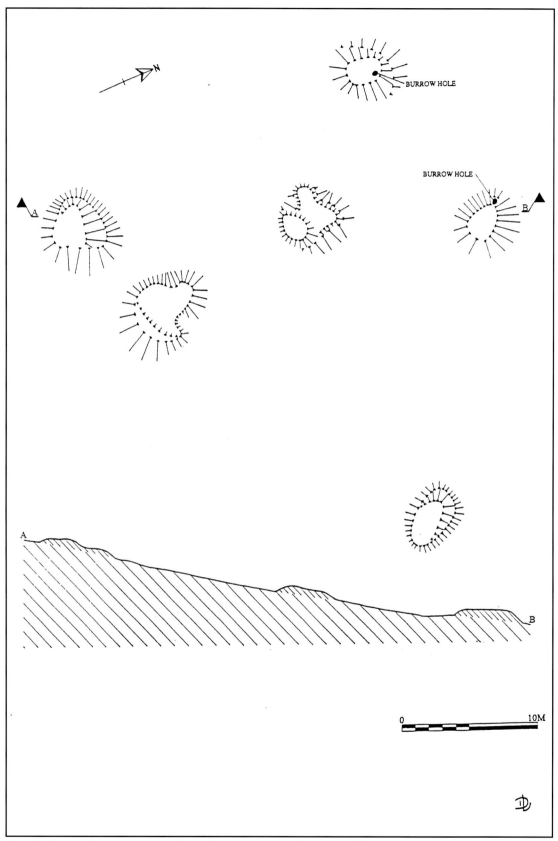

Fig. 5: A possible cemetery of burial mounds in Bellataleen (11).

11 Bellataleen – Mounds (group)
O.S. 87:10:6 (4220 1960)
Site 106 OD 91-122
Fig. 5
Situated in an area of cut-away bog between Croagh Patrick and the shores of Clew Bay. A group of six apparently earthen mounds occur within an area of 40 metres square. All but one is still well defined, and they average 5m wide and from 1.2m to 1.6m in height. These were uncovered following turf cutting and all are cloaked in heather. Local folklore connects them with the burning of peat for the provision of ash to apply to impoverished ground. A presence of ash in its composition may consequently be inferred. There is a possibility however that these mounds may be of more recent date.

12 Carrowmacloughlin – Mound
O.S. 87:9:3 (1645 2361)
Site 096 OD 30-61
Set on a low drumlin, this mound of earth and stone measures 7.7m N-S by 8.5m E-W and reaches 1.7m in height. Livestock have slightly scarred the outer edge of the site.

13 Killeencoff – Mound
O.S. 87:16:3 (9112 1464)
Site 104 OD 61-91
Near the centre of a field of good grazing, which was referred to in times past as 'The Lawn' (landowner). Roughly circular mound of earth and stone 5.1m N-S by 5.9m E-W and 1m high at most. Formerly faced with stone around the edge, only two stones now remain. Flat on top, it measures 3.5m N-S by 4.2m E-W. This site is referred to locally as a fort.

14 Kilsallagh Lower – Mound
O.S. 86:12:5 (8065 1995)
Site 023 OD 15-30
Located in a meadow not far from the seashore, this mound of earth and stone is 8m across N-S and E-W and from 0.55m to 1.3m high. Partly overgrown, it is referred to by the landowner as a 'lisheen'.

15 Leckanvey – Mound
O.S. 87:9:1 (0140 2325)
Site 114 OD 0-30
Irregularly shaped mound or tumulus with a later field fence along its S end, where it is lowest. It measures 11m N-S by 9m E-W overall while the flat top is 9m N-S by 6m E-W. The maximum height is 1.3m at N. The interior contains three circular hollows, 5m to 7m in diameter, 2m to 2.5m across internally and 0.3m deep on average; these appear likely to represent the sites of cists, similar to those from many of the cairns in the Burren area, Co. Clare.

16 Leckanvey – Mound
O.S. 87:9:1 (0255 2295)
Site 095 OD 0-30
Very similar to the other mound in the townland (15). Composed of earth and gravel, it is roughly circular and 17m in diameter and reaches a maximum height of 2.2m at W. Two round hollows 1.5m in diameter and 0.25m deep are situated in the E sector, while a third is also evident at E.

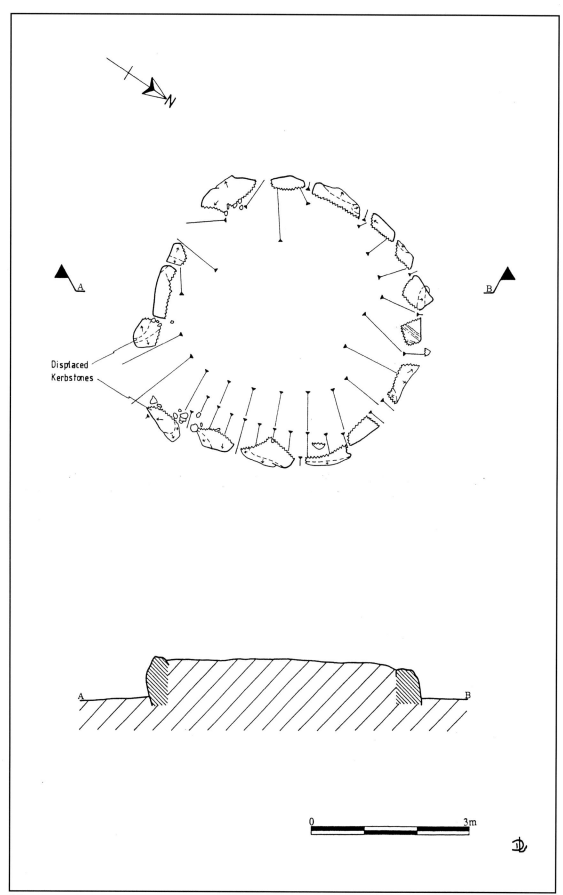

Fig. 6: Stone lined mound in Murrisknaboll (18).

17 Leckanvey – Mound
O.S. 87:9:5 (0790 1582)
Site 062 ✔ OD 91-122
Sheeroe
Plate 22b
This impressive mound dominates the landscape on the Leckanvey side of Croagh Patrick. While it primarily resembles a natural drumlin, it is nevertheless remarkably regular in appearance. It is more elongated than circular, aligned NW-SE, and is steepest along N at 15m. An insignificant erratic on top is split in three. A few hundred metres to W stands a similar type natural mound. Its prominence in the landscape and the translation of its name as 'the red fairy hill' warranted its inclusion in the list.

18 Murrisknaboll – Mound
O.S. 87:11:1 (4731 2633)
Site 059 OD 15-30
Fig. 6 + Plate 30a
In a slightly uneven field of pasture with a wonderful view of Croagh Patrick. Small circular stone-lined mound of earth 5.4m in diameter and from 0.5m to 1m high. A total of 16 stones from 0.3m to 0.62m in height enclose the mound and some smaller packing stones are visible between them.

19 Streamstown – Mound
O.S. 87:8:5 (8050 3262)
Site 10501 OD 0-15
Near the roadside, close to sea level and within a poorly preserved enclosure (238). A large mound of earth and stone roughly 14m in overall diameter – flat on top where it is 7m across. It varies in height from 0.6m along E to 2.2m between S and W where some recent digging was carried out. A small-scale excavation close to the N limits of the site failed to yield any dateable material (Bennett [ed.] 2000).

20 Thornhill – Mound
O.S. 87:9:2 (1235 2910)
Site 011 ✔ OD 0-30
Plates 23a + 23b
Impressive, almost circular tumulus with an overall diameter of 18m, while the flat-top is 9m across. It varies in height from 1.8m (E) to 2.5m (S) and is constructed of earth and stone. A later cruciform pillar of stone and mortar, containing a millstone, was erected on top to celebrate Catholic Emancipation in 1824. The tumulus lies at the N end of a crescent-shaped enclosure 36m N-S by 30m E-W overall; its mainly earthen bank is practically level internally and from 1m to 1.5m high externally, while site interior is too uneven to have been used for habitation. It appears to be directly associated with the tumulus, though possibly of a much later date. An Admiralty Chart dated 1898 names a turret at this site, though one suspects they confused the cruciform pillar with one.

21 Carrowmacloughlin, Glencally, Teevenacroaghy – Cairns
O.S. 87:13:6 (2050 0210)
Site 04303 ✔ OD 610-640
Roilig Mhuire
Plate 4
These cairns form the third station of the Croagh Patrick pilgrimage and are located along the W base of the cone of Croagh Patrick, on level ground, where four townlands meet. Clear views are afforded only to the S. Three impressive cairns stand here in an irregularly shaped enclosure (220). Roughly aligned NE-SW, the largest at SW end is 11m across with the remainder from

Plate 4: Aerial view of cairns (21) and associated enclosure (220).

5.5m to 6.5m in diameter. They vary from 1.8m to 3.2m in height. Their outer layers are formed of small loose stones, probably from later religious visitations, and each has a stone platform or berm outside their southern half. Its name connects it with the Virgin Mary and reinforces its importance as part of the stations of the Reek. This name also suggests a possible Early Christian settlement within the large enclosure (220) here.

22 Sheean – Cairn
O.S. 88:3:4 (4935 5230)
Site 018 ✔ OD 91-122
Prominently sited on a ridge with exceptional views of central, and particularly western, Mayo. The core of the monument is mostly of stone but earth is more prominent around its outer slopes. This enormous cairn reaches 4m high above field level, and its overall dimensions measure 23m N-S by 18m E-W. A trigonometrical station occupies its highest point while its interior is currently hollow. A distinct but shallow fosse 4m wide is evident outside its W half. Beside it to the N is a rectangular damp hollow 17m N-S by 15m E-W internally. The hollow is enclosed by a bank which is 1m high externally, 1.6m high internally and is an impressive 9m wide at the base; this is more than likely associated with the cairn; its flat top averages 1.5m wide.

23 Teevenacroaghy – Cairn
O.S. 87:14:5 (3160 0320)
Site 045 ✔ OD 488-518
𝕷𝖊𝖆𝖌𝖍𝖙 𝕸𝖎𝖔𝖓𝖓𝖆𝖎𝖓
Plate 20b
On flat ground near E base of the cone of Croagh Patrick, with a commanding view only to the S. This irregular cairn measures 7m N-S by 10.4m E-W and is between 2m and 3m high. Earlier maps show it on the N edge of Casan Patrick (143; the ancient pilgrimage path leading to the summit) – this track has been re-routed farther to the N, and a more recent penitential cairn has replaced this one as part of the modern Croagh Patrick Stations.

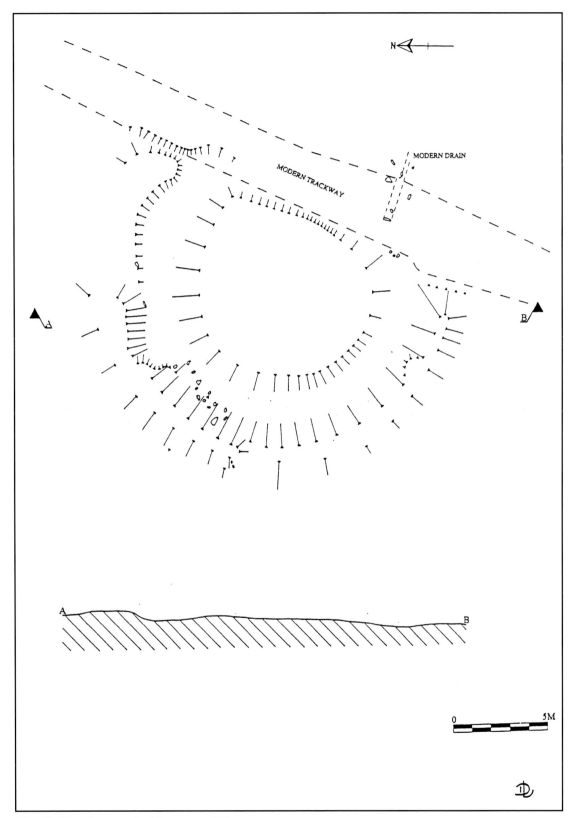

Fig. 7: Ring barrow in Liscarney (25).

24 Letterbrock – Ring Barrow
O.S. 97:12:4 (7120 1600)
Site 011 ✔ OD 91-122
Lissaphuca

Prominently situated on a low drumlin with the tip of Croagh Patrick visible to NNW. This well preserved circular ring barrow is defined by a central mound 20m across and from 0.7m to 1.1m high, which is encircled by a damp fosse 1m wide. An earthen, stone-lined bank with daub and gravel through it forms the outer limits; this bank averages 5m wide overall, and varies from 0.4m to 1.1m high internally and from 1.2m to 2.6m high externally. Some stones line its poorly defined entrance 1.3m wide in E. The overall diameter of the site is 27m.

25 Liscarney – Ring Barrow
O.S. 98:5:5 (0800 3620)
Site 02201 OD 91-122
Fig. 7 + Plate 7b

High on a broad ridge with a wonderful vista to the W. A tall orthostat stands 27m away to SW (57). This circular ring barrow, with an overall diameter of 19m, is partly damaged along E limits by a modern trackway. Its central mound is flat on top and measures 8m across while overall N-S reads 10.5m. An encircling fosse averages 1.5m wide at base. Outer bank is more stony, from 2.7m to 3.3m wide at base while it averages 0.3m high externally and from 0.3m to 0.5m high internally.

26 Moyhastin – Ring Barrow
O.S. 88:10:2 (3215 2715)
Site 116 OD 61-91

This site consists of a ring barrow whose central mound is oval in appearance. It measures 8m N-S by 6m E-W across the top; however, its overall dimensions both read 12m and it reaches 1m high at most. The encircling fosse varies from 1m to 3m wide and is deepest externally along NW at 1.1m. The outer bank has been removed, scarped or covered over by clearance stones. The overall diameter is 20m.

STANDING STONES 27-61

Standing stones are among the most numerous of the monuments in the area, and few have ever previously been mapped by the Ordnance Survey. Generally considered to date from as early as the Bronze Age (Waddell 1998), it is not known when the practice of erecting standing stones discontinued. While the function of any particular standing stone might not be understood without excavation, such sites are thought to either (a) mark burying places (Twohig and Doody 1989), (b) mark ancient boundaries (Cooney 1996), or (c) have featured in some ritualistic or ceremonial occasions (Corlett 1998, 15). The same can be suggested of the stone rows and stone alignments, while there is also the possibility of an astronomical connection with some (ibid., 13-5).

What is now classified as a hut site at Gortbraud, Killadangan (129) was named Standing Stones on the earlier 1840 O.S. map, while (site of) is included on the later map editions of 1901 and 1920. Surprisingly, none of the other orthostats that form a scattered group here in Gortbraud (38) were represented or named on any map, apart from a stone row of four uprights which was termed 'cromlech' (37). The only other stones to be represented cartographically are one in an enclosure in Knappaghmanagh (234) which was moved around the middle of the nineteenth century, and a second one in Lanmore (52) close to the ancient Togher Patrick and named Clogh Patrick.

The most accessible and well known orthostats are a group by the roadside in Killadangan (37 and 38). One of these (37) forms a stone alignment running NNE-SSW. It has been observed on the shortest day of the year that the setting sun disappears into a niche in the mountainous skyline to the SW, when viewed from here.

All the group here, but two, are defined as upright stones put standing by man. The two exceptions are at Killeencoff (45) and at Killaghoor (40) where surrounding stone was quarried away leaving a solitary pillar standing in each location. Nearly all of the stones are composed of schist while their distribution and siting are varied. Orientation does not appear to have been important, with no one alignment being noticeably favoured. Of particular note and interest is the large concentration to be found in the Killeencoff townland area, where the most prominent member (44) at 3.55m is also the tallest. One local person referred to an upright pillar stone, which reputedly stood in Glaspatrick graveyard (251) very many years ago, but which was seemingly broken and moved.

Stone pairs occur at Carrowmacloughlin (30), Fahburren (33) and Letterbrock (55) with a widely-spaced three-stone alignment at Murrisk Demesne (58) while one stone of a probable alignment survives at Liscarney (57). Askillaun townland ten miles to the W contains a well-defined double stone row (Corlett 1997, 79) and further tall orthostats occur near the coast in its general vicinity.

Standing stones are believed to have been used in some of the rites associated with the inauguration of a king during the early Historic period and were looked on as phallic symbols. The king who was quasi-divine underwent a symbolic mating with the local earth goddess (O'Rahilly 1946). The Feast of Tara has been shown as a fertility rite which deified the king (Binchey 1958) and similar feasts probably occurred at Navan, Cruachain (Mytum 1992, 57) and Croagh Patrick.

All descriptions following are for single standing stones unless otherwise stated.

27 Boheh (E.D. Knappagh)
O.S. 97:4:6 (9114 5025)
Site 026 OD 61-91
At the highest point of a field dominating the view to W. Located just S of the only example of rock art from the region (1) and the Togher Patrick (144). A tall stone 2.08m high, it is slightly pointed at the top and somewhat rounded at the base. It is 1.13m wide and 0.66m thick at most. Known locally as the 'tall stone'.

28 Carrowbaun
O.S. 88:5:6 (1825 4065)
Site 102 OD 30-61
Just above and on the SW edge of Westport town, this stone is 1.65m high and is set in a slight irregular mound. The mound edge is missing from NE to SE while its overall NNE-SSW diameter is 14m, reduced to 10m across top. Aligned WNW-ESE, the stone is 1.7m wide and 0.8m thick at most.

29 Carrowbaun
O.S. 88:5:6 (2220 3693)
Site 113 OD 30-61
This stone on SE slopes of a low drumlin is a conglomerate, composed of schist and white quartz. Aligned NNE-SSW for 1.45m, it is 1.5m high and 0.75m thick.

30 Carrowmacloughlin – Stone Pair
O.S. 87:9:5 (1230 2222)
Site 097 OD 30-61
Situated on the N slopes of a ridge, these stones lie 6.9m apart. Both are aligned N-S and average 0.8m high, 1m wide and 0.5m thick. There is a slight hummock beneath the stone to the N. Both stones form a WNW-ESE alignment.

31 Cloonagh
O.S. 87:12:5 (8076 1653)
Site 086 OD 122-152
Practically concealed by heather and scrub, this stone of schist and white quartz is 0.9m high, 0.85m wide and 0.32m thick. Aligned WNW-ESE, it is triangular in plan and tilts slightly to NE. Particularly scenic views from here.

32 Cloonmonad
O.S. 88:5:1 (0661 4300)
Site 030 ✔ OD 0-30
Plate 14a
This orthostat 1.5m high and wide and up to 0.88m thick is surrounded by modernity, in the midst of Springfield Housing Estate. Another nearby orthostat is contemporary with the modern housing.

33 Fahburren – Stone Pair
O.S. 87:11:6 (6616 1532)
Site 078 OD 91-122
Fig. 8
Old disused cultivation ridges surround these stones on all sides. This pair of standing stones aligned WNW-ESE stand 14m apart. Both are regular in appearance, and some low set stones between them may be associated. That to E is 1.26m high, 0.4m thick, 0.48m wide on top and 1.05m wide at the base. The second stone is 1.48m high, 0.35m thick and from 0.3m wide at the top to 0.9m wide at the base. Locally referred to as a 'giant's grave'.

34 Farnaght
O.S. 88:13:2 (1510 1510)
Site 094 OD 30-61
Aligned NW-SE for 1.2m, it varies from 1.3m to 1.5m high and reaches 0.52m thick. Situated on a SW facing slope in a stony, boggy area.

35 Glencally
O.S. 97:1:2 (0915 5610)
Site 045 OD 152-183
This stone 1.8m high is aligned N-S for 1.3m and is 0.6m thick. It lies on the steep S facing slopes of the Glencally hills in a rather inaccessible area. It leans gently to the S and narrows at the top on its face.

36 Glinsk
O.S. 97:8:3 (8715 4328)
Site 043 OD 91-122
In an area of much rock outcrop and scrub, this low stone is only 0.4m high. Aligned NE-SW, it is 0.95m wide and 0.21m thick. Both the NE and SW ends of the stone are pointed with the former also naturally serrated.

37 Killadangan – Stone Alignment
O.S. 87:11:2 (6095 2738)
Site 01402 ✔ OD 0-15
Cromlech
Fig. 4b + Fig. 21 + Plate 8b
Four orthostats aligned NNE-SSW form a stone row 5.5m long. Tallest stone is 1.05m high and all average 0.8m wide. Three recumbent stones lie at its S end. Earlier cartographic evidence suggests that more stones formed part of this structure. This stone row lies within an oval-shaped bivallate enclosure (231). Late in the year, it has been observed that the setting sun disappears behind a dip in the mountain skyline, directly in line with the SSW end of this alignment.

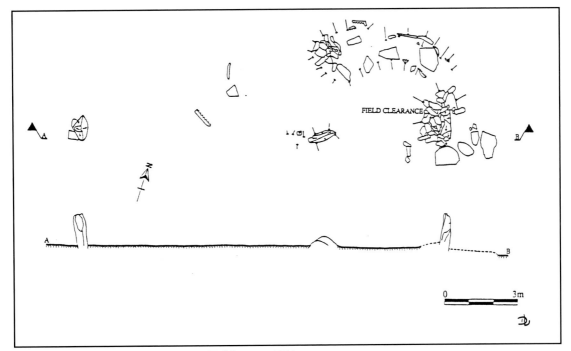

Fig. 8: Pair of standing stones in Fahburren (33).

43

38 Killadangan – Group of Standing Stones
O.S. 87:11:2 (6000 2710)
Site 01407 ✔ OD 0-15
Fig. 21

This random group of orthostats stands close to the sea shore and is constantly attacked by high water tides. A nearby bivallate enclosure (231) containing a stone row (37) was possibly also associated with these stones, though Corlett argues for a late date for the enclosure (J.I.A. 1998). A bank (64) runs N-S through part of this low-lying area (see fig. 26).

Stone A is aligned NE-SW, it stands 1.23m high, is 0.95m wide and 0.55m thick at most.

Stone B stands on the E edge of a bank (64) and drain. Tilting slightly to E, it is aligned NE-SW and 1.33m high, 0.9m wide and 0.3m thick; there is a smaller orthostat near it to E.

Stone C stands 5m to W of the bank (64) and drain. It is aligned N-S, 1.1m wide and 0.5m thick and 1.3m high. It tilts to the NW.

Stone D is 45m to W of the bank and drain and stands 1.6m high, 0.8m wide NNE-SSW and 0.7m thick. Within 12m to SE of this stone are the foundations of a stone hut (129).

Two stones at E (on plan) are not very clear and while well embedded into the ground, reach only 0.45m high at most.

39 Killadangan
O.S. 87:12:1 (7282 2381)
Site 076 OD 0-30

This orthostat was removed from its socket a number of years ago and now lies prostrate beside it. The stone measures 1.45m long, 1m wide and 0.32m thick, while the socket is round and 0.5m deep at present.

40 Killaghoor
O.S. 88:6:1 (2745 3833)
Site 090 OD 30-61

This huge conglomerate was left when surrounding stone was quarried away (similar to no. 45 in Killeencoff). It is 2.6m high, 3.8m wide E-W and averages 0.7m thick. A large seam of white quartz runs along the S face near the base. It lies near the highest point of a low drumlin.

41 Killeencoff
O.S. 88:9:4 (0220 1990)
Site 109 OD 61-91

On the heather-covered N slopes of a hill stands a rectangular limestone boulder aligned NW-SE, 1.1m high, 1.66m wide and 0.34m thick. A smaller stone at SE end helps to support it. The stone also contains white quartz.

42 Killeencoff
O.S. 88:9:4 (0105 2005)
Site 114 OD 30-61

This roughly rectangular stone is aligned N-S and is 1.15m high, 1.2m wide and 0.36m thick. It tilts slightly to E. Situated on N slope of a hill.

43 Killeencoff
O.S. 88:9:4 (0100 1912)
Site 04802 OD 61-91
This large irregular limestone block is also set on the N slope of a hill. It is aligned NW-SE, is 1.58m high, 0.8m wide and 0.95m thick. It was partly covered with heather.

44 Killeencoff
O.S. 88:9:4 (0150 1842)
Site 097 OD 61-91
Here a limestone upright 1.43m high is incorporated into a drystone field wall. It is 1.2m wide N-S and 0.28m thick.

45 Killeencoff
O.S. 88:9:4 (0300 1995)
Site 098 OD 61-91
Plate 27a
In a fine commanding location, this piece of rock was left standing while stone from all around it was quarried away. It is aligned E-W and is 3.55m high and 1.05m thick. Numerous boulders and flags near its N and W edge appear to have possibly formed part of some ancient structure – perhaps of a megalithic nature.

46 Killeencoff
O.S. 88:9:4 (0270 1778)
Site 100 OD 30-61
This prominent upright aligned N-S is only 0.45m high at S end but reaches 1m at N. In plan it is five-sided and it measures 1.45m wide and 0.8m thick at most.

47 Killeencoff
O.S. 87:12:6 (8652 1819)
Site 103 OD 61-91
This orthostat is of limestone, stands 1.25m high and is 0.58m thick. Aligned N-S, it is 0.9m wide and slightly pointed at the top. A few smaller stones at its E edge suggest the stone was possibly part of a larger feature.

48 Kilsallagh Lower
O.S. 86:12:6 (8890 1555)
Site 021 OD 61-91
Located on high ground in an area of cut-away bog, this impressive stone is aligned N-S and is 1.3m high, 1.4m wide and 0.38m thick. It is leaning to the W. A small natural hollow is visible near the top of the W face.

49 Kilsallagh Lower
O.S. 86:12:5 (7755 1518)
Site 022 OD 30-61
This irregular standing stone is located 12m W of a deep mountain stream. Aligned ENE-WSW, it is 1.3m high while it reaches 0.96m in width and in thickness.

50 Knappaghmanagh
O.S. 88:13:2 (1390 1082)
Site 05701 ✔ OD 61-91
Standing Stone (site of)

It is recorded by Knox (1904) that this orthostat, which was very long, was reputedly taken about 1850 to make a lintel for a new church at Knappagh. No such stone can be identified at St. Thomas Church, Knappagh today. The stone was situated within a large enclosure (234) which cannot be traced on the ground surface today.

51 Laghloon
O.S. 97:4:1 (7757 5630)
Site 051 OD 91-122

Standing in a partly boggy area, this impressive stone 1.35m high is aligned NNE-SSW and is 0.2m thick. Roughly rectangular in shape, it leans slightly to E.

52 Lanmore
O.S. 98:1:3 (2420 5765)
Site 00201 ✔ OD 91-122
Clogh Patrick

This standing stone is situated in a poorly preserved enclosure 200m to the N of Togher Patrick (144). It is aligned N-S and is 2.4m high, 2.4m wide and 0.2m thick. It leans sharply to the N and is almost pointed on the top. It is known as Clogh Patrick.

53 Lanmore
O.S. 98:2:1 (2380 5443)
Site 027 OD 91-122

This stands about 100m to the S of Togher Patrick (144). It is aligned NNE-SSW and is 1.53m high and 0.3m to 0.6m thick. The top is slightly pointed.

54 Lenacraigaboy
O.S. 87:10:5 (3638 1942)
Site 084 OD 91-122

This stone is aligned NW-SE and is 1.25m high and 0.55m thick. It is slightly pointed on top. Evidence for underground water action is evident around this location.

55 Letterbrock – Stone Pair
O.S. 97:16:1 (7290 1505)
Site 056 OD 91-122

On top of a low drumlin, these two uprights stand 1m apart and are aligned N-S. That to S is incorporated into a wall and measures 1.46m high, 0.93m wide and 0.3m thick. Its counterpart tilts to the W and is 0.88m high, 0.65m wide and 0.33m thick.

56 Letterbrock
O.S. 97:12:4 (7490 2189)
Site 059 OD 91-122

Standing 14m from a ringfort (217) on a drumlin surrounded by bog, this stone is aligned N-S and is 1.1m high and 0.26m thick. A piece of the top is broken off.

57 Liscarney
O.S. 98:5:4 (0786 3600)
Site 02203 OD 91-122
Plate 27b

This impressive orthostat, near the centre of a reclaimed field, is aligned NNE-SSW; it is 2.06m high, 1.78m wide and from 0.7m to 0.9m thick. A natural oval hollow is evident at the top of the stone; this varies from 0.08m to 0.27m deep. Landowner claimed that there were other orthostats in this field, but he had them removed.

58 Murrisk Demesne – Stone Alignment
O.S. 87:10:2
(3540 2624) Site 054
(3734 2591) Site 055
(3800 2592) Site 056
OD 0-30

Near the N base of Croagh Patrick and not far from the shore of Clew Bay. This stone row is aligned ENE-WSW.

The stone furthest to W (054) is 1.4m high, 1.47m wide at the base and up to 0.22m thick. It is set into a slight hummock 0.4m high, 4.9m across N-S and 3.6m across E-W.

The second stone (055) is 25m to ENE of the first. It is 1.65m high, 0.5m thick and leans toward the SW.

The third stone (056) stands 122m to E of the last one. Also aligned NE-SW, it is only 0.7m wide at the base but reaches 1.5m wide higher up. It is 1.35m high and 0.28m thick. Lying 60m to NNW of this, a boulder in the field and some exposed rock 15m to SW of the middle stone may have been associated with the alignment.

59 Oughty
O.S. 97:11:5 (5830 1760)
Site 044 OD 122-152

This field surrounded by flowing water contains a small upright 0.8m high. It is 0.64m wide WNW-ESE and up to 0.28m thick; this stone is triangular in plan.

60 Owenwee
O.S. 97:4:2 (7560 5391)
Site 048 OD 91-122

On the S slopes of a drumlin, this standing stone is aligned NE-SW and is 0.83m tall, 0.8m wide and 0.28m thick.

61 Streamstown
O.S. 87:12:2 (8015 2984)
Site 111 OD 0-30

This insignificant looking stone near the roadside is aligned WSW-ENE and is 0.82m tall, 1.2m wide WSW-ENE and 0.67m thick. It appears to be broken.

276 Brackloon
O.S. 87:16:6 (8752 0480)
Site 124 OD 60-91

Within Brackloon Wood, this irregular stone is 1.3m to 1.5m high, 1.25m wide and 0.3m thick. It is aligned NNE-SSW. Just 32m to W is a taller stone of similar width and thickness, but up to 1.8m tall; this stone tilts to N and E. Slight doubts exist concerning the authenticity of their antiquity.

ANCIENT FIELD FENCES 62-65

As with so many other monuments within the survey, ascribing an exact, or even rough date for these boundary fences is difficult. Composed of either stone or earth, or a combination of both, four separate sites were identified. Only in Owenwee townland (65) can the system of fences be definitely seen to lie under a considerable layer of peat – though much of this has been cut away.

Research and excavation beneath the bog at The Céide Fields in North Mayo has uncovered field systems which date back to our first farmers in the Neolithic times (Caulfield 1989). The Neolithic period witnessed the arrival of agriculture and the first permanent residences constructed by our ancestors.

It is likely that the pre-bog walls at Owenwee date to prehistoric times, while some artifactual evidence or carbon-dateable material from this site would obviously help in the dating. In Boheh (62), a series of mainly stone banks have two cashels (147 and 153) and a ringfort (203) on their outer perimeter, while a large number of circular huts (95-102) and one fulacht fiadh (69) lie within the area of these fences. Turf was also cut at the area around this site and indeed the damp ground of today is still ideal for the formation of bog. So extensive was the turf cutting or erosion at Carrowmacloughlin (63) that the surviving banks in the field system are set mainly on uneven denuded damp ground. The system in Killadangan (64) may be contemporary with the enclosure here (231) and possibly pre-dates any of the standing stones from here (38), as two of them have been erected on its edge.

62 Boheh (E.D. Kilsallagh)
O.S. 96:8:2 (826 425)
Site 046 OD 30-91
On poor quality damp ground sloping to N in an area of numerous hut sites, forts of stone and earth and a fulacht fiadh. Stone spreads representing former fences are to be found haphazardly throughout an area measuring roughly 500m N-S and E-W. This system probably extended eastwards where there are further hut sites and two cashels.

63 Carrowmacloughlin
O.S. 87:9:5 (1500 1850)
Site 069 OD 61-122
Various field fences 1.5m to 2.5m wide and composed mainly of stone and earth form a field system on NW foothills of Croagh Patrick. None exceed 0.5m in height and the system extends 250m N-S by 60m E-W.

64 Killadangan
O.S. 87:11:2 (6050 2720)
Site 01406 OD 0-30
Fig. 21 (K on plan)
Two main banks, primarily earthen, could be identified here. One running from the S of a bivallate enclosure (231) is best preserved, averaging 1.5m wide and 0.5m high. The second lies to the W of the same enclosure and is not as well defined. A drain along its W edge appears more likely to be the result of frequent marine action at the site. Two orthostats (B on plan) were put standing on this bank. Tidal activity may have removed similar-type banks in this low-lying area.

65 Owenwee
O.S. 97:7:3 (6550 4230)
Site 049 OD 91-122
Fig. 9
Low wall foundations 0.3m high at most and from 0.8m to 1.4m wide were uncovered here following turf cutting. The walls lie on a thin layer of soil above the bedrock and they cover an area which extends 120m N-S and 55m E-W. All wall foundations run fairly haphazardly through the area

with the longest visible stretch of wall reaching 19m long NE-SW and with a nearly circular outline of stone and earth 5m across, near the northern end. Uncut bog near the N of the site possibly contains a continuation of this system. Land to the W is forested and landowner stated that a fulacht fiadh was exposed and then removed during planting.

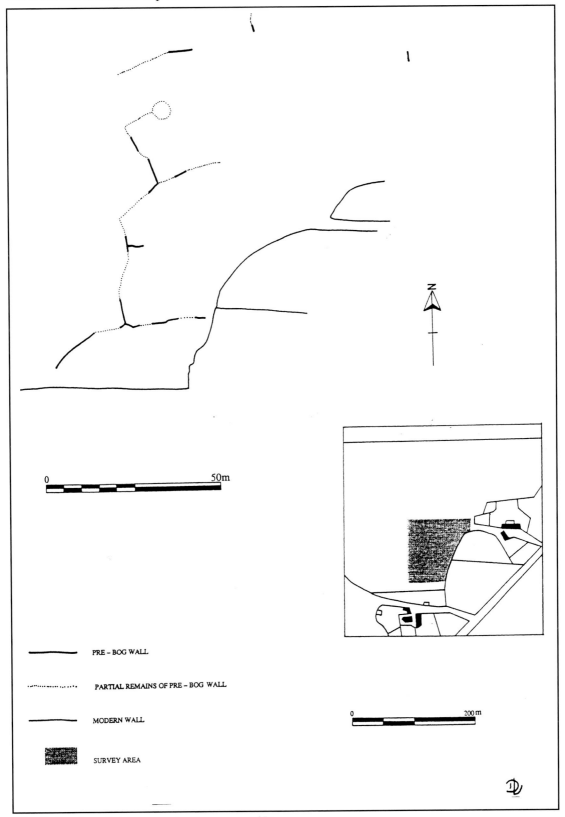

Fig. 9: Pre-bog field system in Owenwee (65).

FULACHT FIADHA 66-92

This site type is being detected or uncovered in greater numbers than any other monument type from around Ireland. Paradoxically it is only through destruction that many are originally identified, as instanced by examples at Brackloon (72), Lanmore (90) and Liscarney (91); at Brackloon, burnt stone spreads following clearance indicated several such sites, while the cleaning of drains in Lanmore and Liscarney exposed burnt stone and ash on the drain sides.

The general consensus in Irish archaeology is that they were used as cooking places for meat – the residual stones and ash being the by-product of boiling water by immersing heated stones in it. In Irish the word 'fulacht' translates as 'cooking place' while 'fia', though it translates directly as 'deer', is also according to many scholars an abbreviated form of the 'Fianna', with whom they are commonly associated in early literature. After each 'cooking' at the site, the burnt stone, ash and cinders were removed from the cooking trough and cast aside. Their dispersal was generally in a fan-shape and resulted in the classic fulacht fiadh taking the outline of a horse-shoe. A major detailed survey in the Turlough Parish of Co. Mayo in 1987 identified 120 such sites (Lawless 1987, 32-36). Charcoal from many sites around the country generally place them securely in the Bronze Age, and a C14 date of 3005 ± 110 BP was obtained recently from one in Knappaghbeg (87). A much earlier date of 2590 BC was obtained from one in Ballinrobe (Walsh 1994). However, their use up to medieval times is shown by the discovery of rotary querns in the body of occasional fulachta fiadha, while a medieval cooking trough was excavated in Waterford City in 1987 (Buckley 1990, 47-8). In general, the bulk of excavated examples appear to be of Bronze Age date. In the New Survey of Clare Island 1991-95, archaeological fieldwork recorded forty-two definite fulacht fiadha, twenty-two of which survive fully or partially intact (Gosling 1993, 9).

The list of 27 sites given below are nearly all on or beside a water source. Some 50% are located below the 60m contour, with 30% between 120 and 210m. As a rule, fulacht fiadha are visible as fertile green mounds in otherwise infertile damp areas. However, presumably on account of the poor soil fertility and the wet nature of the terrain, most of the local examples are covered by heather or moss and thence are not immediately evident or obvious to the eye. It may also be that these examples are located in relatively isolated places where the bog is actually regenerating itself and the associated vegetation has already thrown its cloak over many of them.

66 Barragleanna
O.S. 97:1:5 (1180 5235)
Site 038 OD 152-183
Fig. 10
Near the SE edge of a mountain stream on the isolated S slopes of Croagh Patrick. Here two sidestones of the original cooking trough reaching 0.48m high are still *in situ*, while a third lies in the adjacent stream. Overall the site measures 8m NNE-SSW by 3.9m wide and its cooking area faces N. It reaches 1.2m above the level of the water along W and slightly less elsewhere. One of the few examples of the cooking trough still visible, if only partially.

67 Bellataleen
O.S. 87:6:6 (4561 1864)
Site 05802 OD 91-122
Within 1m of the E edge of a mountain stream, this horseshoe-shaped example measures 12m N-S by 9m E-W overall, while it varies from 0.8m to 1.3m high. Its depressed cooking area, measuring 3m long and 3.4m wide by about 0.5m deep, faces SW, and a later wall is built through it at W.

68 Bellataleen
O.S. 87:11:4 (4625 2023)
Site 06302 OD 91-122
Fig. 11 + Plate 9b

Exposed stone at this site, which measures 7m N-S by 10.2m E-W, is all sandstone. It is a well preserved, classic-shaped example between 0.6m and 1.2m high. The depressed cooking area with an original sidestone 0.1m high in SW corner faces W and measures 2.65m long by 2.9m wide.

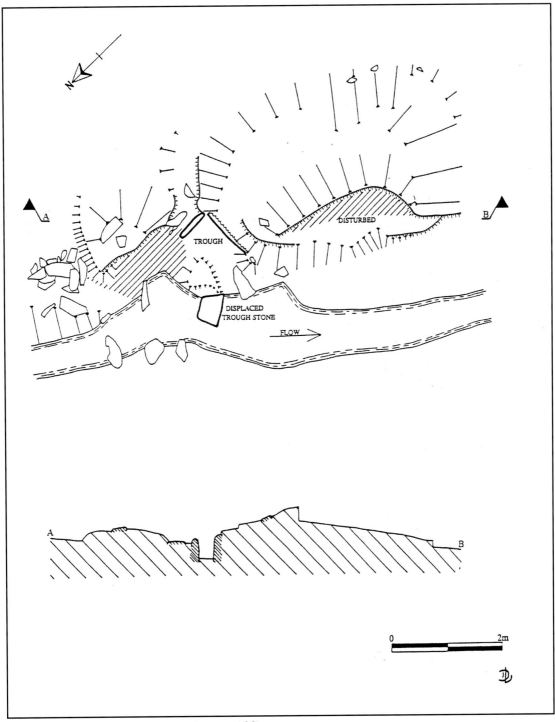

Fig. 10: Fulacht fiadh in Barragleanna (66).

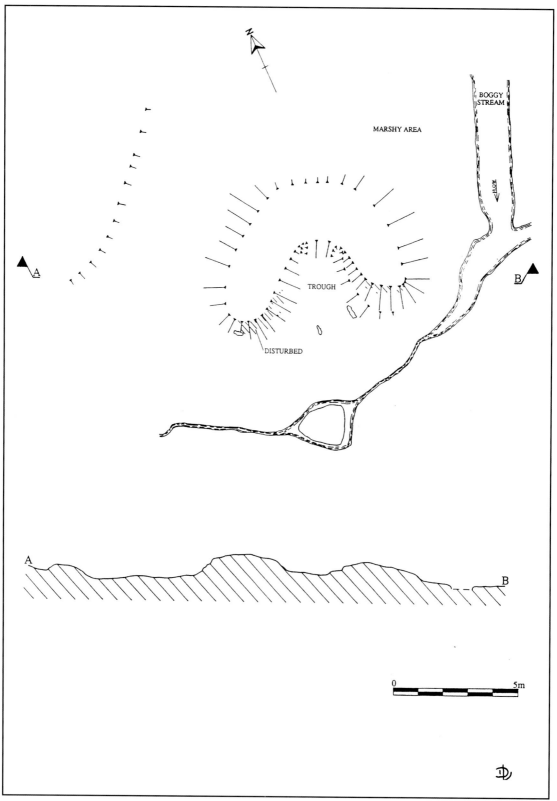

Fig. 11: Fulacht fiadh in Bellataleen (68).

69 Bellataleen
O.S. 87:11:4 (4639 1730)
Site 082 OD 122-152
Irregular in shape, this is formed of two hummocks of burnt stone 8m long NNW-SSE, 3.9m wide and 0.9m high at most. A hollow area between the hummocks probably indicates the location of the trough. The site lies at the confluence of two small streams.

70 Bellataleen
O.S. 87:11:4 (4723 1544)
Site 083 OD 152-183
A low green fulacht fiadh 4.5m NNE-SSW by 6.9m wide lies adjacent to a stream disappearing underground. It stands 0.65m high at most and with no clear trace of a cooking hollow.

71 Boheh (E.D. Kilsallagh)
O.S. 96:8:2 (818 421)
Site 052 OD 30-61
Appears to face SE, it has maximum overall dimensions of 7m. In section along the stream it is 1.3m high above water level but much lower elsewhere.

72 Brackloon
O.S. 87:16:3 (8952 1290)
Site 118 OD 30-61
In a partly cleared damp field, a large area 15m across in diameter contains spreads of burnt stone and ash. Five separate concentrations 0.3m deep at most are probably individual sites.

73 Cahernamart – Possible Fulacht Fiadh
O.S. 88:5:3 (1615 4168)
Site 03202 OD 0-30
Oval-shaped, elongated raised green area 17m E-W by 9m wide in damp surroundings. Stands up to 1.5m high along S. No trace of a cooking trough and no clear evidence of any burnt stone at the site.

74 Carrowbaun
O.S. 88:5:3 (1880 3812)
Site 101 OD 30-61
Beside the junction of two modern roads, this measures 9.4m NNE-SSW by 6.5m wide and reaches 0.5m high along N. The cooking hollow faces W, is 3m long by 1.8m wide and is 0.3m deep at most.

75 Carrowbaun
O.S. 88:5:5 (1442 3420)
Site 105 OD 30-61
A kidney-shaped example measuring 14.2m NNE-SSW by 12.6m wide. Its depressed hollow area faces W and measures 5m long, 4m wide and 0.7m deep. Cut by a later wall, it stands 0.6m to 0.9m high.

76 Carrownalurgan
O.S. 88:5:5 (0950 3480)
Site 107 OD 0-30
Poorly preserved fulacht fiadh 12.8m NNE-SSW, 11m wide and up to 0.8m high. Clear identification of the cooking area is not possible due to its indistinct outline. Another possible cooking site 7m across and 0.56m high lies 20m away to WNW.

77 Cloonmonad
O.S. 88:5:2 (1280 4022)
Site 111 OD 0-30

On the edge of a former turlough or small lake, this is represented by a low hummock 0.6m high at most and 5.5m across. The trough area faces SE and measures 2.7m by 1.9m wide and 0.3m deep at most.

78 Drumminaweelaun
O.S. 87:5:3
(8744 3775) Site 09801
(8810 3750) Site 09802
OD 0-30

Two poorly preserved sites in a damp marshy area.

9801 to NW is 9m NE-SW by 9.7m wide and 0.5m high. Trough area 0.15m deep is represented by a band of rushes, 3.2m long by 2.4m wide, and faces SW.

9802 to SE is slightly better defined; 12.5m NW-SE by 8.8m wide and 0.65m high at most. Shallow cooking area 4.9m NE-SW by 2m wide is again rush filled.

79 Glaspatrick
O.S. 87:9:6 (2144 2165)
Site 090 OD 30-61
Plate 5

This well preserved example lies close to a mountain stream and reads 17.7m N-S by 11.5m wide and 1.35m high. Depressed trough area faces W and is 8m E-W, 4.5m wide and up to 0.6m deep; there are two set stones on the E edge of this cooking area.

80 Glaspatrick
O.S. 87:10:1 (2772 2401)
Site 091 OD 30-61

Horseshoe-shaped in plan, this measures 10.2m NNE-SSW, 6.5m wide and from 0.4m to 0.8m high. The cooking depression faces NW and is about 2m across.

81 Glencally
O.S. 97:1:1 (0742 5335)
Site 041 OD 122-152

Surviving as a mound of burnt stone 8.3m NW-SE by 4.3m wide on the edge of a stream, it is highest along NW at 1.15m. A hollow area facing SW may indicate the trough.

82 Glencally
O.S. 97:1:2 (0848 5372)
Site 047 OD 122-152

This poorly preserved example faces NE away from the adjacent stream. Overall dimensions measure 4.3m NW-SE, 3m wide and average 0.35m to 0.5m high; however along SW the top of the mound is 1.4m above the water level in the stream.

83 Killadangan
O.S. 87:11:1 (6114 2692)
Site 01404 OD 0-15

An irregular low hummock of some burnt stone 5.3m N-S by 5.8m E-W rises to 0.4m high. A roughly circular SE facing hollow 1.5m across probably marks the site of the former cooking area.

84 Killaghoor
O.S. 88:6:2 (3165 3815)
Site 092 OD 0-30

An irregularly shaped spread of burnt stone and ash 0.55m high at most, 5.6m NW-SE and 5.2m wide. No clear cooking hollow. Water in the adjacent turlough at NE has caused erosion to the site edge though the main body of the site is intact.

85 Killaghoor
O.S. 88:6:4 (2315 3685)
Site 104 OD 30-61

This site takes the form of a grassy mound 1.3m high between SE and N. Elsewhere it blends in naturally with an adjacent gravel ridge. Overall dimensions are 14.2m N-S by about 8m across. No clear cooking area evident.

86 Killeencoff
O.S. 88:9:4 (0347 1552)
Site 099 OD 30-61

Though low, only 0.5m high at most, this displays an obvious horseshoe shape. Its N-S and E-W dimensions read 10.6m across while rushes fill the SW facing trough area; this measures 4m long by 3m wide.

87 Knappaghbeg
O.S. 88:14:1 (2272 1164)
Site 095 OD 30-61

This example, which measured approximately 5m NW-SE by 6.5m wide and stood 0.6m high, was removed through reclamation a good number of years ago. Charcoal recovered from here at the time yielded a date of 3005 ± 110 BP

88 Lanmore
O.S. 98:4:3 (1810 4060)
Site 028 OD 91-122

Here is a fine example, 21m NE-SW by 12m wide and from 1m to 1.3m high. The N facing cooking hollow is 4.6m long, 3m wide and up to 1.1m deep. A few stones embedded into the top at E are unburnt.

89 Lanmore
O.S. 98:4:6 (1565 3605)
Site 037 OD 91-122

Another well preserved site, 13m NE-SW by 10.6m wide and from 0.6m to 1.1m above ground level. It is open to NW where its hollow measures 3.7m long, 2.6m wide and 1m deep at most. No clear sign of a water source.

90 Lanmore
O.S. 98:1:6 (1745 4815)
Site 034 OD 91-122

A small stretch of burnt stone and charcoal is visible on the sides of a drain. It is only visible in section and is 0.35m deep at most.

91 Liscarney
O.S. 98:5:1 (0290 4090)
Site 035 OD 91-122

Like the last one, this only became evident after clearing the sides of a drain. The drain has bisected the fulacht fiadh, and the preponderance of burnt stone and ash is visible on the W face. It stretches for 7m N-S and averages 0.5m thick.

92 Pollanoughty
O.S. 97:14:3 (4548 1160)
Site 040 OD 61-91

This was levelled by machinery so the present spread 8.7m N-S by 6.3m E-W may be a bit exaggerated. A slight hollow 1.5m to 2m across probably indicates the cooking trough area.

273 Glaspatrick
O.S. 87:10:2 (2800 2420)
Site 121 OD 30-61

A late discovery. Close to the church and graveyard in Glaspatrick lies this large area of grass covered burnt stone 14m N-S by 12m E-W and up to 0.6m high at most. Its cooking area 4m N-S by 2.5m E-W and 0.3m deep faces a stream to S.

Plate 5: One of the three newly discovered fulachta fiadha in Glaspatrick (79).

Plate 6a: Some of the survey team.
Left to right: (front) Martina O'Kane, Carol Killeen, Siobhán Duffy; (2nd row) Dwayne Jordan,
Rowena Keane; (3rd row) David Loftus, Grainne Byrne: (4th row) Leo Morahan,
Will Williams; (back) Will Igoe, Richard Gillespie.

Plate 6b: Croagh Patrick Archaeological Committee in Murrisk.
From left: Owen Campbell, Cathal Hughes, Breeda Hyland, Gerry Walsh, Paddy Foy,
Harry Hughes, Very Rev Michael Molloy, John Groden, Leo Morahan, Liam Walsh R.I.P.,
Jarlath Duffy, Seán Staunton. Member absent from the photograph: Michael Gibbons.
Committee Patrons: Most Rev Michael Neary, Archbishop of Tuam and
Most Rev Joseph Cassidy, retired Archbishop of Tuam.

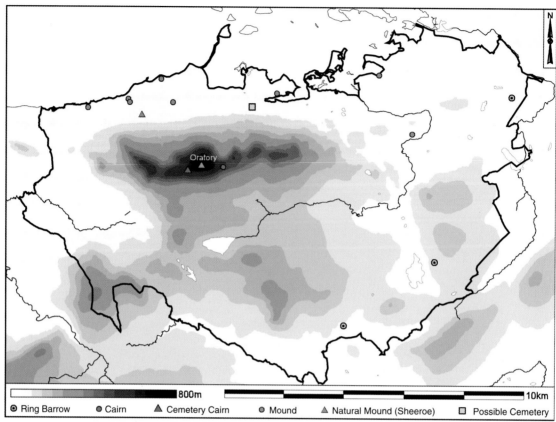

Plate 7a: Distribution of burial mounds, cairns and ring barrows showing the natural mound at Sheeroe and group of mounds which form a possible cemetery in Bellataleen.

Plate 7b: Well defined ring barrow in Liscarney (25).

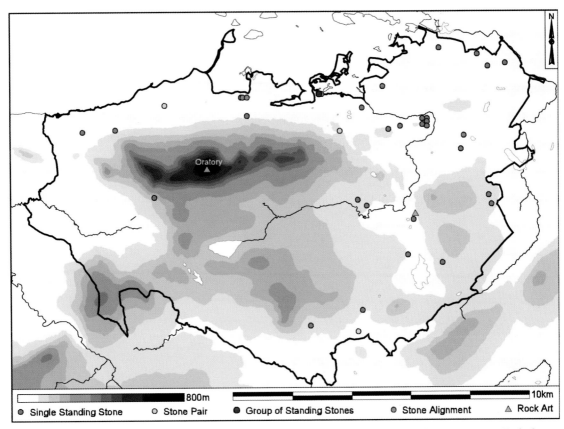

Plate 8a: Distribution of orthostats or standing stones, including the rock art stone at Boheh.

Plate 8b: Stone alignment in Killadangan (37) awaits the setting winter sun.

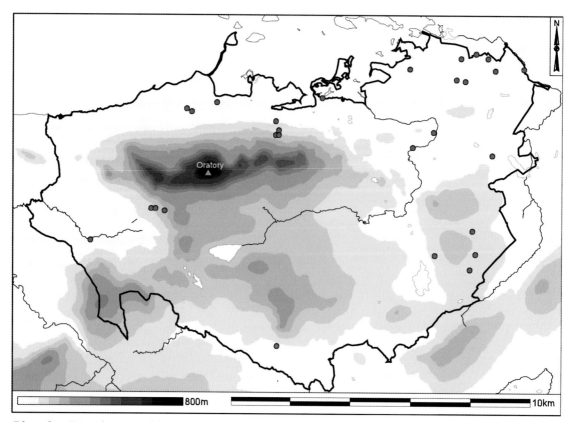

Plate 9a: Distribution of fulacht fiadha within the area.

Plate 9b: Well defined fulacht fiadh beside a streamlet in Bellataleen (68) viewed from west.

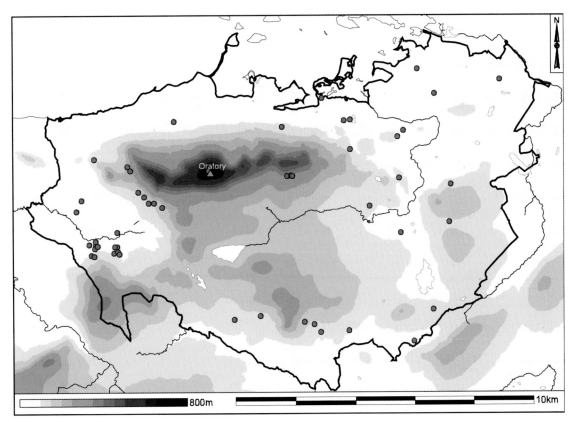

Plate 10a: Distribution of huts or hut sites from the survey area.

Plate 10b: Typical stone hut on a river edge in Durless (119) with the hills of Clare Island visible in the background.

61

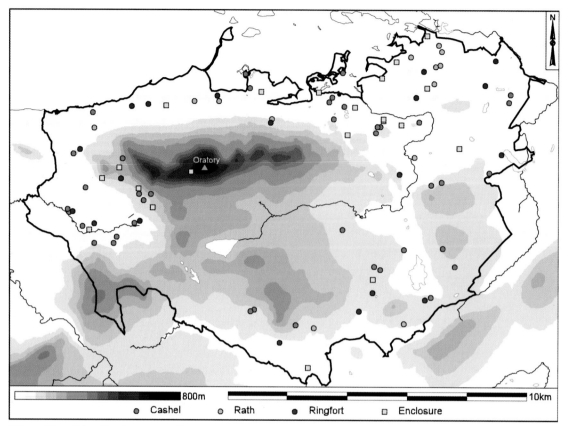

Plate 11a: Distribution map showing cashels, raths, ringforts and other enclosures.

Plate 11b: Surviving portion of a rath on a ridge overlooking Clew Bay in Bellataleen (188). Traces of cultivation ridges are also visible.

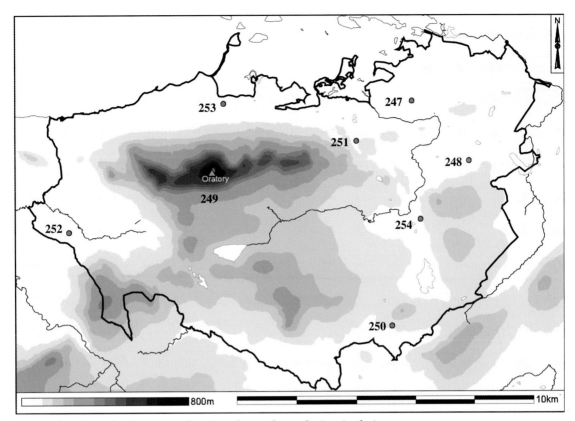

Plate 12a: Distribution map showing the early ecclesiastical sites.

Plate 12b: Aerial view of ecclesiastical enclosure in Furgill (252).

Plate 13a: Ornate Early Christian cross slab in ecclesiastical enclosure at Knappaghmanagh (254 + 269).

Plate 13b: Long cist in Knockfin (7) resembling a megalithic structure; referred to locally as Finn mac Cool's grave.

Plate 14a: Standing stone in Cloonmonad (32).

Plate 14b: One of the large deer folds on high ground in Deerpark West.

Plate 15a: The rock art stone at Boheh (1).

Plate 15b: The NNE end of chamber number one, showing access area from the main passage.

Plate 16a: The south and west wall of the excavated oratory on the summit of Croagh Patrick.

Plate 16b: Overview of oratory remains during excavation, taken from NE. Note doorway in E wall and modern church (1905) in the background.

Plate 17: Geology map of the area.

DX = Deer Park Complex – Serpentinite, talc, schists, metabasite; **DP** = Deer Park Schist Formation – Semi-pelitic schists, basic volcanics; **DM** = Derrymore Formation – Sandstone, slate, tuff, conglomerate; **CoGr** = Corvock Granite – Biotite granodiorite to syenogranite; **LK** = Letterbrock Formation – Sandstone, slate, conglomerate; **FN** = Farnacht Formation – Dacitic to andesitic arc metavolcanics; **Kl** = Killadangan Formation – Mélange with black shale matrix; **DL** = Derrylea Formation – Sandstone, mudrock, conglomerate, tuff; **SH** = Sheeffry Formation – Mudrock, sandstone, tuff; **LN** = Lough Nacorra Formation – Calcareous psammite, quartzite at top; **CB** = Cregganbaun Formation – Quartzite, psammite, basal conglomerate; **DG** = Derryheagh Formation – Calcareous siltstone, marble; **AA** = Aille and Barney Fms (undifferentiated) – Limestone, subordinate shales; **wp** = Westpot Oolite – Oolites and calcareous sandstone; **AI** = Aille Limestone Formation – Dark fine-grained limestone, thin shales; **CR** = Castlebar River Lmstone/L, Akeel Oolite – Sandy oolite, dark limestone and shale; **MO** = Moy Sandstone Formation – Pale sandstone, siltstone, conglomerate.

HUT SITES 93-143

Small circular houses or hut sites generally tend to be the principal internal features from numerous forts, as witnessed at several local examples (146, 157, 159, 162, 166 and 196 amongst others). However where these huts occur independently, they are treated of as a separate site type (O'Riordáin 1971). The majority of field surveys from around Ireland are recording such monuments, which give internal diameters of between 3 and 6m and whose plans are invariably nearly circular.

Most notable in this regard from Co. Mayo is a group of six in the Aghamore area near Ballyhaunis (Byrne et al 1991, 77-79). Among the most satisfying aspects of the Croagh Patrick Survey was the location of 51 sites in this category. Research excavation at one in Glenbaun (124) by Grant and Loughran has certainly provided interesting results and evidence of activity there (Bennett [ed.] 1992 and 1993, 47-8, 61). Prior to excavation it had resembled most of those classified as huts in this chapter with a 1.5 to 2m wide earthen bank, faced occasionally with large stones internally and externally. Excavation within the interior revealed several pits of various sizes containing charcoal and iron slag. Recovery of furnace bottoms from the interior conclusively shows that the primary, if not the only activity at the site was iron smelting; an 8m long stone-lined feature running from the east interior to the bank in N and continuing to the exterior may be interpreted as an associated flue (ibid.). Whether this monument and the other members of this category were purpose-built for the smelting of iron, or whether pre-existing huts were adapted for such use, is not clear. However the enclosing bank in the S sector of the excavated example in Glenbaun was constructed later than the industrial activity and comprised several layers of ash and baked clay.

Another circular hut on a drumlin in Killadangan is named Curreenaneeran Fort on O.S. maps; as this translates as 'the little hill of the iron', perhaps it could indicate the original activity carried out at the site. In spite of the above findings, it is assumed that the majority of these monuments were utilised for habitational rather than manufacturing purposes.

Most huts conform roughly to the same size, averaging 3 to 5m in internal diameters and with enclosing banks of earth and stone from 0.3 to 0.9m high. Stone facing in the bank, using large slabs, is a feature of the better preserved examples in most of the townlands. Huts occur in twenty-eight separate townlands but distribution varies greatly, with notable concentrations in the Bouris, Durless, Cuilleen, Glenbaun and Glencally areas. They can occur at any altitude and just half are located between 30 and 90m above sea level. Three huts stand between sea level and 30m, with a further three between 270 and 300m. The remainder of the huts are between 90 and 270m.

Whatever their dating, it cannot escape attention that the vast majority are located in close proximity to ringforts or similar-type enclosures. To show the relationship between these huts and the forts, the following is a list of sites which have a ringfort or enclosure not more than 200m away, with most in much closer proximity.

Hut no.	For/Enclosure no.	Hut no.	For/Enclosure no.
146, 188 & 201	93	117, 125	163
95, 118, 119, 120, 121	161	126, 128	164
96, 97, 98, 99, 102	147	127	166
100, 101, 124	203	129	231
104	148	132	211
107	205	133	177
109, 137	153, 155, 225	134	207
110	200	136	25
114, 115	159	140	199
116	173	142	186, 187

93 Bellataleen
O.S. 87:11:4 (4780 1886)
Site 112 OD 91-122

On high ground, surrounded by damp heather and rush-covered land. This hut measures 5.1m N-S by 6.15m E-W overall, internally reduced to 2.8m N-S by 3.5m E-W. Its enclosing bank is mainly earthen, 1.8m wide at most, and while it is practically level externally between S and N, it averages from 0.5m high internally and externally elsewhere. Interior hollow with rushes forming a concentric band 1m wide just inside bank. No clear entrance.

94 Bofara
O.S. 87:16:3 (8365 1414)
Site 089 OD 61-91

High on a drumlin with extensive views from NE to SW and within 5m of townland boundary to E. Enclosed by a moss-covered wall 0.25m to 0.6m high, though generally lower internally, and reaching 2.1m wide at most. The entrance is marked by a gap 1.3m wide in the S. Internal diameters measure 3.5m N-S by 2.7m E-W.

95 Boheh (E.D. Kilsallagh)
O.S. 96:8:3 (8814 3905)
Site 02101 OD 91-122

On the E shoulder of a steep ridge, overlooked between E and N but with a fine aspect elsewhere. Consists of a conjoined hut aligned NNE-SSW enclosed by banks of stone and earth with no clear entrance. The more northerly is better preserved with internal diameters of 3.8m NNE-SSW by 3.4m WNW-ESE (5.8m overall). It displays good internal facing 0.5m high between SE and E and the enclosing bank reaches a maximum height of 0.8m in the N half (and that externally). The enclosing bank of its southerly component is barely evident in the NE quadrant and averages 0.5m high elsewhere; its internal diameters both read 2.5m while the E-W overall diameter reads 5.4m.

96 Boheh (E.D. Kilsallagh)
O.S. 96:8:2 (8246 4297)
Site 036 OD 30-61

On a flat terrace on the N slopes of a steep ridge and surrounded by lazy beds. This sub-circular hut has internal diameters of 8m N-S by 6.5m E-W; overall 15m N-S by c. 18m E-W. Enclosed by a stony delapidated spread 3.7m wide on average; 0.25m high internally and 0.6m to 1m high externally. No facing in evidence, while interior is hollow and occupied by three lazy beds. Where a fence meets it at E, this creates an increased width to the bank.

97 Boheh (E.D. Kilsallagh)
O.S. 96:8:2 (8188 4077)
Site 044 OD 61-91

On a slight terrace of a N-facing ridge with best views from W to E. This roughly circular hut is 3.3m N-S by 2.9m E-W internally and overall 5.3m N-S by 5.6m E-W. Enclosed by a bank of stone and a little earth, with internal facing 0.4m high in most sectors. Gaps occur but seem to have been caused by livestock. There is a noticeable increase in the width of the wall at W. Just outside NW sector is a poorly preserved oval hut 3m N-S by 4.5m E-W overall.

98 Boheh (E.D. Kilsallagh)
O.S. 96:8:2 (8201 4107)
Site 047 OD 61-91

Two poorly preserved roughly circular huts, almost conjoined. That to E is enclosed by a stony spread 2.5m wide on average and measures 5.5m in overall diameters; a regular band of irises outside at S suggests an associated feature. That hut to W is at a slightly lower level, with internal diameters of 5m and a bank 0.3m high at maximum.

99 Boheh (E.D. Kilsallagh)
O.S. 96:8:2 (8249 4269)
Site 048 OD 30-61

The remains of a hut 3m N-S by 4m E-W internally. Best defined along S where earth and stone bank averages 1m wide, 0.55m high externally and 0.4m high internally. A low curving scarp forms the edge elsewhere.

100 Boheh (E.D. Kilsallagh)
O.S. 96:4:5 (8100 4729)
Site 049 OD 30-61

Near the northern end of the townland on a gentle S-facing slope. Much overgrown hut with one diameter measuring 7m NW-SE overall, reduced to 5.2m internally. Enclosing bank of stone and earth is much denuded, exposing large stones in many sectors. It reaches its greatest height on the exterior at the N (0.7m) while a gap 1.3m wide in the E probably represents the entrance. Interior is overgrown and partly waterlogged, with a sunken stone-lined feature 0.7m across in the SW sector.

101 Boheh (E.D. Kilsallagh)
O.S. 96:4:5 (8127 4795)
Site 050 OD 30-61

This lies 100m to the NE of the last hut on slightly drier land. Poor remains of an oval-shaped hut with internal diameters of 5m N-S by about 2.4m E-W and about 6m across overall. Enclosing element of earth and stone averages 1.5m wide, 0.45m high internally and 0.45m to 0.75m high externally. A large stone 0.8m high at the E forms rough inner facing.

102 Boheh (E.D. Kilsallagh)
O.S. 96:8:2 (7940 4182)
Site 051 OD 30-61

At N end of a steep rocky incline, this small oval hut is only 1.8m N-S by 3m E-W internally. Enclosed by a stone spread 1m wide, 0.2m high and with a later wall built on it.

103 Boheh (E.D. Knappagh)
O.S. 98:1:5 (1940 5040)
Site 033 OD 122/152
Fig. 12

Near the eastern edge of the townland in a generally infertile area. A plain circular hut 4.6m N-S by 4.1m E-W internally bordered by a bank of earth and stone; some of its stone has been stained and cracked by heat. Its enclosing bank is flat on top (1m wide) and best preserved in the S half at 3m wide, 1.1m high externally and 0.6m high internally. A lowering to the bank in the E suggests the entrance location.

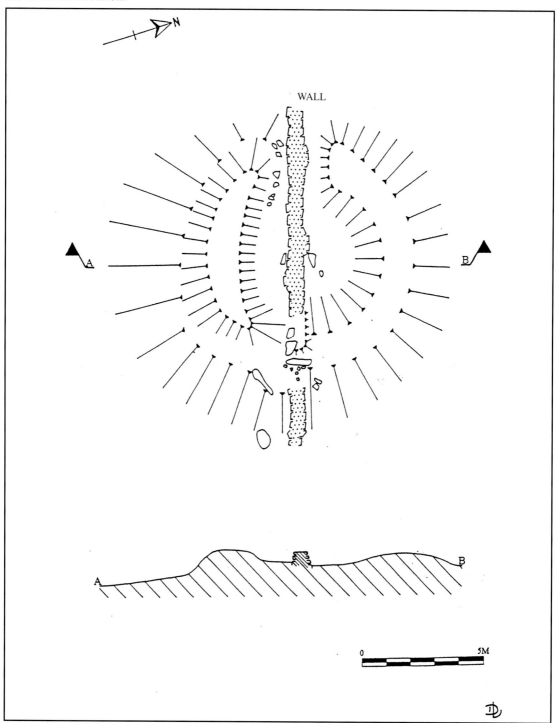

Fig. 12: Hut site in Boheh (E.D. Knappagh) (103).

104 Brackloon
O.S. 87:16:6 (8428 0172)
Site 085 OD 91-122

On a small terraced area surrounded by undulating rocky ground. Roughly circular hut 5.5m N-S by 6.5m E-W internally and 8m overall. Low enclosing wall has occasional inner and outer facing 0.1m high at most and 0.7m thick. There is a later wall built on its W sector, while a small break in the SSW indicates the entrance.

105 Carrowbaun
O.S. 88:6:4 (2365 3481)
Site 103 OD 61-91

In an area of poor quality undulating grazing with little shelter. Poor remains of a hut with internal diameters of 6m N-S by 6.8m ENE-WSW. Enclosed by a collapsed wall spread 1.8m wide at most and 0.3m to 0.4m high which only survives from the S to ENE.

106 Carrowmacloughlin
O.S. 87:9:5 (1303 2050)
Site 066 OD 61-91

This lies at a point where improved grazing meets with heather-covered mountain. A bank of stone and earth 2.5m wide only survives from E to W. It averages 0.5m high internally and from 0.3m to 0.8m high externally. None of the bank in the N half can be seen while a gap 0.8m wide in the W probably marks the entrance. The E-W diameter is 11m internally and 15m overall. A later wall running E-W cuts the site in two.

107 Carrowmore
O.S. 98:9:1 (0415 2430)
Site 02302 OD 91-122

On the NE facing slopes of a ridge with good views from W to SE. Oval-shaped hut measuring 4.5m N-S by 6.8m E-W internally. The enclosing bank of stone and earth forms a spread 2.2m to 3.3m wide and between 0.8m and 1m high externally. A later lime kiln was built into the bank in the SE sector.

108 Carrowrevagh
O.S. 97:16:3 (9030 1335)
Site 018 OD 61-91

On slightly raised ground surrounded by bog. This stone-lined hut measures 4.5m across in internal diameter. Stone facing 0.6m wide, 0.25m high internally and 0.4m high externally is found in the N sector. The interior is rubble-filled.

109 Cartoor
O.S. 96:4:4 (7562 5150)
Site 033 OD 30-61

On the E side of a small valley in a field of rushy grazing. The NE half of a small hut survives. Enclosed by a bank of stone and earth 1.5m wide on average, reaching 0.4m high externally and 0.7m high internally. Some few facing stones 0.35m high are visible internally and externally while a short stretch of walling 0.25m high survives in the NE. The internal NW-SE diameter is 3m and the SW half has been removed.

110 Cloghan
O.S. 87:8:6 (8891 3613)
Site 099 OD 0-30
On a slight rise in an undulating area of rushy land. Overlooked by a pronounced ridge from NW to NNE. Stone-lined hut whose enclosing wall averages 1m thick. Inner facing stones are more plentiful than those externally and average 0.4m high. External facing reaches 0.55m high and is best defined from W to E. Enclosing element survives throughout apart from ESE sector. Badgers have burrowed into this site.

111 Crott Mountain
O.S. 87:15:4 (5014 0180)
Site 115 OD 274-305
On the southern slopes of Crott Mountain near the E edge of a mountain stream. Small hut 3m NW-SE by 2.3m NE-SW internally with a gap 0.7m wide in the SSW. Enclosing bank of stone and earth is from 1.4m to 2.1m wide and averages 0.3m to 0.6m high.

112 Crott Mountain
O.S. 87:15:4 (4996 0205)
Site 116 OD 274-305
Located 11m to the NW of the last site in a similar setting. Small hut 3.4m N-S by 2.1m E-W internally with the hint of a second conjoined one outside to N. Its bank of earth and stone reaches 0.4m high at most and it averages 1m wide at the base.

113 Crott Mountain
O.S. 87:15:4 (4892 0171)
Site 117 OD 274-305
On the S side of Crott Mountain with an excellent view downslope. There are two hut sites 5m apart here. Both are enclosed by banks of earth and stone. That to the E measures 2.8m N-S by 1.9m E-W internally; its bank averages 1m wide and it varies from 0.15m to 0.4m high. The hut to the W is almost D-shaped and measures 3.3m N-S by 2.6m E-W internally. A gap 0.9m wide in the ENE was the likely entrance. Dimensions of bank are similar to its easterly neighbour.

114 Cuilleen
O.S. 86:16:6 (9145 0545)
Site 019 OD 213-244
On a slight earthen plinth on the W and SW slopes of Ben Goram. This hut 3.8m N-S by 4m E-W internally is enclosed by a wall of stone mixed with earth. Most stones are large and set on their edge, averaging 0.5m high internally. The enclosing wall itself averages between 0.8 and 1m in width and in external height. Its S interior contains a pear-shaped hollow 0.4m deep with internal readings of 2m N-S by 1.8m E-W. Known locally as the 'Dane's Yard'.

115 Cuilleen
O.S. 86:16:6 (9180 0385)
Site 027 OD 213-244
A clearly circular spread of stones 6m across overall and 3m internally. Low facing stones in many sectors reach only 0.15m high. No original wall thickness.

116 Cuilleen
O.S. 96:4:2 (7702 5541)
Site 042 OD 30-61

A small, roughly circular stone hut 4m in internal diameters, lies on the gentle S slope of a valley. Enclosed by a stony bank 0.4m to 0.7m high and 1.2m wide on average. Bank is lowest from N to E.

117 Cuilleen
O.S. 97:1:1 (0320 5840)
Site 052 OD 122-152

Near the SW end of Ben Goram in a stony mountain area. This site close to the townland boundary is a conjoined hut, with the northern part well preserved; its bank displays good inner and outer facing 0.65m high at most and from 0.6m to 0.9m thick. Internal diameters measure 4m N-S by 3.4m E-W, with a small gap in the SW. Adjoining its S sector is a roughly circular hollow 3m across, enclosed by a low bank; this bank is gapped at NW.

118 Durless
O.S. 96:8:3 (8902 4011)
Site 02002 OD 61-91

In a well sheltered depression on the edge of a stream in the W of the townland. Circular hut 5m across internally. Enclosed by a bank of collapsed stone 1m wide on average with some facing evident, which reaches 0.35m high in the N interior and 0.25m in the W exterior. A gap in the ENE is the only entrance.

119 Durless
O.S. 96:8:3 (8917 3925)
Site 02102 OD 61-91
Fig. 13 + Plate 10b

Very well preserved circular hut with internal diameters of 4.5m and overall diameters of 7m. Some fine original inner and outer facing survives, up to 0.6m high. Two stones in the inner face at N and one at W are of greater than normal dimensions for such a site – up to 1.4m long and 0.4m to 0.65m high. An original wall thickness of 1.2m was obtained in SSE. No clear entrance, it lies adjacent to a stream.

120 Durless
O.S. 96:8:3 (8831 4140)
Site 035 OD 61-91

Roughly circular hut 5m N-S by 4m E-W internally. Enclosing bank of stone and earth gapped for 2m at W (possibly original). This bank is of great width at E, though some or all of this may be natural. It averages 3m wide and 0.8m high with some inner facing along S.

121 Durless
O.S. 96:8:3 (8818 4140)
Site 034 OD 61-91

Clear outline of a circular hut 4m across internally. Enclosed by low inner and outer facing 0.85m apart on average. Situated 20m from the last hut.

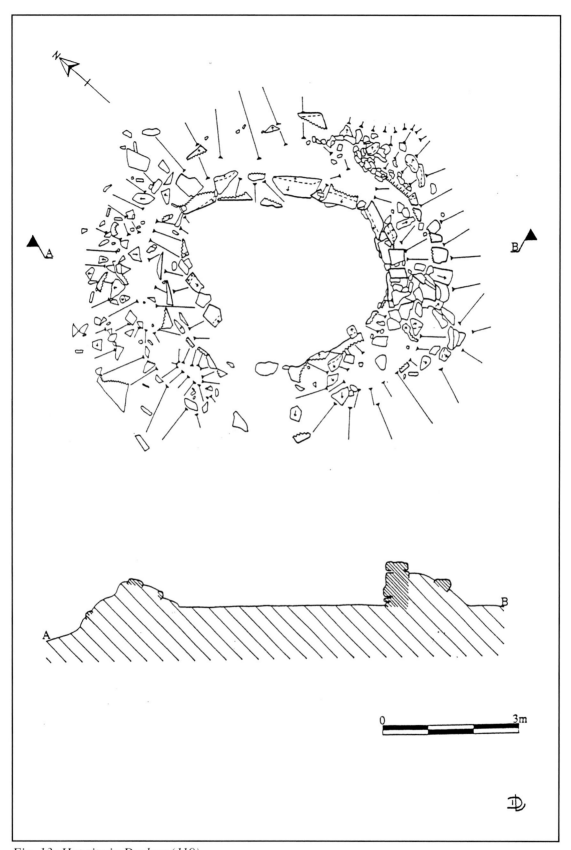

Fig. 13: Hut site in Durless (119).

122 Fahburren
O.S. 87:11:6 (6533 1956)
Site 107 OD 61-91
Poorly preserved, oval-shaped foundations 6.5m in overall dimensions. Enclosed by a collapsed wall 1.5m to 2m thick but with no clear facing; it reaches 0.3m to 0.7m high and there is no sign of an entrance.

123 Fahburren
O.S. 87:16:1 (6861 1204)
Site 087 OD 122-152
On the E shoulder of a ridge with excellent views to the N and E. Poorly preserved hut 3m across internally with a gap 1m wide at the E. Collapsed enclosing bank of stone reaches 0.8m wide and is from 0.2m to 0.6m high, while rock outcrop forms some actual facing.

124 Glenbaun
O.S. 96:4:6 (8822 4605)
Site 028 OD 30-61
In a field of mixed fertility, this sub-circular hut is still basically intact in spite of partial excavation. Overall diameters of 8.5m decrease to 5m N-S by 4.2m E-W internally. Enclosing bank of stone and earth reaches 0.55m high at most. Excavation results are indicative of this being used as an iron working site (Bennett (ed.) 1992 &1993).

125 Glenbaun
O.S. 97:1:1 (0470 5630)
Site 00102 OD 122-152
Another classic hut site, circular in shape and 4.5m across internally. Built of earth and stone, much of the stonework in the enclosing bank is cyclopean in form. Original wall thickness is 1.05m in N, and inner facing 0.3m to 0.9m high is more vertical than its outer counterpart (which is much scarcer). External height of bank varies 0.8m to 1.1m, and the entrance 1m wide is situated in SW. The hut is beside a stream at S base of Ben Goram.

126 Glencally
O.S. 97:1:2 (0830 5475)
Site 00202 OD 122-152
On well elevated ground on S slope of Ben Goram. Close to a stream with a nearby cashel to the S (164). Classic circular hut 4m across internally, enclosed by a bank of large stones and earth. Stone facing is clearest internally reaching 0.75m high in the E half. Externally the bank varies in height from 0.6m in E half to 1.3m in W half. An original wall thickness of 2.6m was obtained in the W. Present opening in the S may be original.

127 Glencally
O.S. 97:1:1 (0625 5350)
Site 035 OD 91-122
Within 10m of a mountain stream in an infertile, partly sheltered area and with a nearby cashel to the N (166). Poorly preserved hut with internal measurements of 3.6m N-S by 3.2m E-W. Enclosing bank of stone and earth averages 2m wide and reaches 0.8m and 1.1m in maximum internal and external height respectively – the bank is absent between W and N.

128 Glencally
O.S. 97:1:2 (1450 5335)
Site 039 OD 122-152

Unfortunately situated on the track of a mountain rivulet today but no doubt much drier when originally constructed. Internally 5.5m N-S by 6.5m E-W, its enclosing bank of earth and stone reaches 3m wide at most. A natural rock face delimits its E and SE sector, while elsewhere the enclosing bank reaches 1.8m and 1.2m in maximum external and internal height respectively.

129 Killadangan
O.S. 87:11:2 (6020 2695)
Site 01405 ✔ OD 0-15
Standing Stones
Fig. 21 [K on plan]

Nearly circular stone hut 14m in internal diameter and least well defined from NW to N. Elsewhere low stone 0.2m high forms the perimeter – some stones along SW are set on edge and form a bank 1m wide. It must remain uncertain what this site looked like originally, and how much its current appearance is due to erosion or interference by man. Certainly there is nothing at the site of an orthostatic nature today as suggested from its name on earlier O.S. map of 1838.

130 Killadangan
O.S. 87:11:6 (6809 2109)
Site 036 ✔ OD 0-30
Curreenaneeran Fort

Excellently sited on the top of a pronounced drumlin with commanding views from NE to SE. Well preserved circular hut with crest-to-crest diameters of 8.7m. Created by digging the interior and forming a bank of earth and gravel from the resultant material. This broad bank averaging 5m wide, 1m high internally and 1.4m high externally is considerably wider and with much less stone than most of the other huts. A banked trackway meets the WNW sector.

131 Killeencoff
O.S. 87:12:6 (8661 1817)
Site 102 OD 61-91

On the N slopes of a steep hill covered with heather. Poorly preserved hut 2.3m N-S by 2.8m E-W internally. Enclosed by a bank of stone with inner facing reaching 0.3m high at most. No clear entrance, and interior appears sunken.

132 Kilsallagh Upper
O.S. 86:16:5 (8145 0740)
Site 024 OD 91-122

This nearly circular hut 4.5m across internally and 7m across overall is best preserved in N half. Internal and external facing stones reach 0.7m high while some of these on the inside are as much as 1m long. No entrance can be seen.

133 Knappaghmore
O.S. 88:13:5 (0875 0205)
Site 115 OD 122-152

Fairly circular hut 6m in internal diameter and over 10m in overall external diameter. Its broad bank of stone and earth reaches 1m high and contains low facing stones at intervals. Along W a natural sheet of rock has been used as the inner edge. A gap of 2.4m at E is probably the original entrance.

134 Knockfin
O.S. 88:9:1 (0380 2940)
Site 087 ✔ OD 30-61

On high ground 50m to the SE of an enclosure containing a megalithic-type structure (7, 235). Well defined circular hut with crest-to-crest diameter of 8m and with an enclosing bank of earth and stone from 2m to 3m wide. Large rocks used in its construction along W where maximum heights of 1.1m internally and 1.25m externally were recorded. A small platform adjoins N sector externally.

135 Lenanadurtaun
O.S. 97:10:5 (3320 2000)
Site 054 OD 122-152

Poorly preserved, circular stone spread 3m N-S by 2.6m E-W internally, and later used as a sheep pen. Only the foundations, which reach 0.25m high, are original. Gap 0.85m wide in NW.

136 Letterbrock
O.S. 97:12:4 (6830 1645)
Site 057 OD 30-61

Low-lying, sheltered area with nearby streams to NE and E. Well preserved hut 4.5m across internally and 8m in overall diameters. Bank is composed primarily of stone and varies from 1.4m to 1.8m wide and from 0.4m to 0.6m in height. Inner facing 0.5m high occurs at intervals. Gap in SSE may be recent.

137 Mullagh
O.S. 96:4:1 (7340 5336)
Site 007 ✔ OD 30-61

Another well preserved, circular hut enclosed by a stony bank; the bank takes the form of facing 0.65m high and 0.9m wide along N. A thickening to the bank at S creates a 'hut within a hut' appearance; the smaller hut is roughly 3.5m across internally by 7m overall while the larger one is 8.5m across overall. Outside the site, a vegetation band suggests a fosse 1.1m to 2.5m wide.

138 Oughty
O.S. 97:11:5 (5380 2102)
Site 036 OD 122-152

A small hut 3m N-S by 2.3m E-W in internal dimensions on the SE slopes of the Oughty hills. Its low bank of stone and earth averages 2.4m wide and while it never reaches 0.3m high externally, it averages 0.6m high internally. Overall dimensions 8m.

139 Oughty
O.S. 97:11:5 (5800 1872)
Site 060 OD 122-152

Yet another hut on high ground near a stream. Measuring 4.3m across internally, its bank, almost exclusively of stone, reaches 0.8m high at most. Larger stone to be found in the bank, mostly in S half. Overall diameters measure 8.5m N-S by 9m E-W.

140 Oughty
O.S. 97:11:5 (6018 1620)
Site 046 OD 122-152

A bank of stone and earth about 2m wide and from 0.3m to 1m high encloses this hut. Some inner facing does exist – one stone in NNE is 0.7m wide and 0.92m tall. Internal diameters are both 4.8m and overall roughly 8m.

141 Owenwee
O.S. 97:4:6 (8560 4710)
Site 029 OD 61-91

Small earthen hut 7.6m across overall and 5m in internal diameter. It is bordered by a bank 1m wide on average and 0.25m high at most.

142 Pollanoughty
O.S. 97:10:6 (4115 2080)
Site 00902 OD 122-152

Equidistant from two cashels which overlook it (186, 187), on O.S. 97. Best preserved along NW, its bank of stone and earth averages 1.1m wide while stretches of stone facing reach 0.25m high. A gap 3m wide in SW seems later. Estimated internal diameters both read 6m. Site interior is surprisingly damp.

143 Summit of Croagh Patrick
O.S. 87
Group of Huts
Site 04405
Fig. 2

A total of at least 13 small stone huts or scoop hollows are located on the summit, to the W and NW of the modern oratory. Not nearly as sturdy or imposing as all the others in this chapter, their outlines vary from circular to oval. Enclosed exclusively by stone spreads 0.5m to 1m wide on average and only 0.3m high; no facing or entrance features are evident. Overall diameters never exceed 6m with dimensions internally varying from 1.5m to 3.5m. There are a further ten probable huts on the summit, represented as slight hollows, some partly stone-lined. Two of the huts were partially excavated by Walsh in 1995 (Bennett [ed.] 1995, 68) and one produced a broken retouched flint flake. This suggests evidence, albeit tentative, that the huts were of an early date.

TOGHER 144

Togher Patrick
O.S. 87, 88, 97 and 98
Site 046 ✔

Trackways or toghers occur in large numbers throughout Ireland and are mainly found preserved in extensive tracts of bog. Ancient trackways as a physical manifestation consist generally of a tough hard material on a softer, often boggy sub-soil. Their construction is usually of wood, which is formed of trunks, planks or branches. The aim was to spread the weight of the people, animals and/or carts on the road over a single large element or several smaller elements, which by itself or combined had a surface large enough to prevent sinking into the sub-soil by upward pressure (*J.I.A.* 1998, 45). Sometimes sand, gravel or flagstones were used to create a smooth road surface. These trackways can be relatively narrow, in which case only pedestrians could use them, or wide enough for wheeled traffic (ibid.).

Dates obtained from timbers indicate more concentrated periods of trackway construction, especially in the Middle Bronze Age. Timbers from a linear structure in Lullymore Bog, Co. Kildare had been worked and provided the early date of 7145 ± 35 BP (ibid.). A catalogue of dates from over 100 Irish trackways concluded that custom-built trackways were designed from an early stage of the Irish Mesolithic, as a response to the occurrence of bogs; that before the employment of draught animals, wide tracks of split timbers were used and that before the shoeing of horses, stone was used in the trackways. Dating of samples from a trackway in Bloomhill, Co. Offaly with an earliest date of 1370 ± 60 BP suggests a construction date of 800 AD or earlier (ibid.).

The only trackway from this survey area is known as the Togher Patrick and is reputedly the route taken by St. Patrick on his way to Croagh Patrick at the dawn of Christianity in Ireland. Croagh Patrick must have been a sacred, much visited place in pagan prehistoric Ireland, and both local and national tradition maintains that St. Patrick felt obliged not only to visit but to remain until he had appeased and converted whatever spiritual power it was believed dwelt there. The Togher Patrick runs westwards for 26 miles from Ballintubber Abbey to Croagh Patrick and in many townlands along the route it has been both represented and named cartographically. Through the intercession of Fr Frank Fahey of Ballintuber over the past fifteen years, the landowners have allowed right-of-way through their lands all along this route; this has enabled pilgrims to avail of a full day's trek from Ballintubber to the Reek, an event which usually takes place a small number of times each year. It passes adjacent to or close to three main early monastic sites at Boheh (019, O.S. 97), Lankill (003, O.S. 98) and Aughagower (063, O.S. 88) with a possible fourth one at Bellaburke (034, O.S. 89). There are numerous other nearby monuments, in particular standing stones and the rock art stone at Boheh (1). No part of the togher appears man-made today though later boreens and roads overlie it in places. The final part of the ascent, on the cone of the mountain, is referred to as Casán Patrick. It is most likely that the togher connected the royal forts of Connaught in pre-Christian times; forts which integrated the Irish word 'cruachan' into their names (Knox 1908, 339) as at Rath Cruachan and Cruachan Aigle (Croagh Patrick). (See next chapter). There is also the possibility that the pilgrim track from Murrisk village to the summit dates back to Christian, or even the pre-Christian period.

HILLFORT 145

HILLFORT RAMPART

Hillforts were principally defensive sites which date back to the Late Bronze Age at c. 1,000 BC. Many are seen as being of ceremonial or religious significance, serving as a tribal rather than a family venue. Physically, it is understandable how Croagh Patrick's summit would be chosen for a hillfort. Pagan significance and beliefs would have attached themselves to its conical peak from the time its environs were first inhabited. The presence of gold locally may also have led to the establishment of a lofty power-base; in such a strategic location control would be assumed over this and all other natural resources. Irish hillforts at Armagh and Downpatrick later developed into towns, while excavations of the hillfort at the latter (which also has a St. Patrick connection) dates it to c. 300 BC.

C. Ottway, who visited the summit of the Reek in 1839, gave a description of the rampart wall for the first time in his book the *Tour of Connaught* (319-20):

> Turning in a northerly direction to where the mountain looks to the north, and presents the longest face of its summit to Clew Bay, I was surprised and gratified to find along this whole range of the platform a low wall, built of large, uncemented stones evidently of the most ancient construction – a Cyclopean monument raised ages before the Roman Patrick ascended, if ever he did ascend, built by that ancient people that have erected their solemn monuments in every land, and have left behind what proves, that however unaccountable their remains, they were created by men of intelligence and great social power. The low wall which, I believe, has never been before noticed, a wall that has borne the Atlantic tempest of thousands of years, I observed, and considered it afforded me a clue to unravel, as I think, the mystery of this mountain, and explain the traditional story of St. Patrick and the serpents…

> Now, what I want to show is, that the Druids had fixed on this sea-over-hanging mountains as their Carmel – thus they had enclosed with their Cyclopean wall, and, no doubt, there were also their circles, and pillar stones, and other monuments, until they were destroyed by their Roman enemies; and it is of little consequence to my position that the Carmelites have now joined the ranks of all-conquering Rome – Rome, that has absorbed and assimilated every former superstition, as Rome civil did every Pagan rite and polity. It does not weaken my argument that the provincial of the Carmelites, now in Ireland, is as little like Elijah as he is like a Druid. Still I maintain that the conquest Patrick achieved was over the 'Sanctos Druides,' and their rites and place – their Carmel – the high place where their honour dwelt.

Present physical evidence, together with this reference, indicate the fortification of the mountain top, though a date for the construction of original walling is unknown. A pre-Christian date for this is suggested by reference to the mountain as Cruachan Aigle (Knox 1908, 26); elsewhere it is stated that at Rathcroaghan the name of cruachan seems to be drawn from the high mound which formed a kind of citadel, within the great rath, and from such a citadel cruachan came to be used as a name for a king's fort (*J.R.S.A.I.* xxxi, 35). Knox also suspected that 'cruachan' was a general name applied to a royal fort (1908, 339) in the period which began not long before the Christian era (ibid., 340). A mingling of the royal blood at both cruachan sites may be arrived at in the reference to Eochaidh, who built the great fort at Rathcroghan, being succeeded as king by Ailill Finn; and Ailill's mother is given as Magu of Murrisk (ibid., 7-8).

145 Croagh Patrick Summit
O.S. 87:14:4 (2560 0430)
Site 044 OD 762-793
Fig. 2 + Plate 2 + Plate 31
Aerial photography (p. 124) shows much of the summit enclosed by a wall which is not very obvious in many sectors at ground level today. Many local people felt that this wall had been the creation of penitents doing their rounds on the summit, in recent centuries. Walsh's 1995 excavation showed that this wall had been regularly constructed along the W and NW, with stone-facing up to 0.6m high internally; there was no overall wall thickness or external height in evidence. These excavations did not embrace the rampart wall along NE, E or S.

This collapsed mountain-top wall appears today as follows:

The collapsed wall spread along N side is only 0.2m high near western end. This increases to 1.2m high near the centre of the wall but decreases again at eastern end; however, no external height could be read on account of the extensive spread to the stones.

Along E the collapsed wall is difficult to make out and survives mainly as a low scarp.

On S side the wall material is best defined at the western end for 45m. Here, it forms a spread about 5m wide, 0.8m high internally and up to 1.6m high externally.

Wall spread at W reaches 6m wide, 0.4m high internally and 2.2m high externally (hollow created externally by removal of surface stones enhances the last measurement considerably). Gap in W wall 2m wide may be original and opens out towards Roilig Mhuire (21). A small cairn to the W of the modern church may be earlier than the enclosing of the mountain top, but so much traffic has passed this way, it is impossible to be certain.

Rough internal diameters of this hilltop enclosure measure 154m E-W and 18m wide at W end.

The arrival of Christianity to Ireland may have brought about the demise of this mountain top enclosure, for, as O'Croinín states, 'the latent violence in most Irish saints' lives with their constant reiteration of the need to do battle with pagan druids and smash them physically if need be reflects the views of Irish Christian writers at the time when they were composed' (1995, 29) and 'there is no reason to doubt that in Ireland zealots took to the high-roads, smashing the symbols of the rival religion and looting its temples' (ibid., 31).

Fig. 14: Sketch of Croagh Patrick and Westport from 1839 (C. Ottway).

FORTS 146-245

CASHELS, RATHS, RINGFORTS, ENCLOSURES and SOUTERRAINS

The most recognisable of Irish field monuments are forts or ringforts and they have served as habitation sites for generations of our ancestors. Usually circular in shape, their construction material depends on the local geology or geography – thence we get forts enclosed by earthen banks (referred to as a rath) and those enclosed by a stone wall (referred to as a cashel). In certain parts of the country, a rath is termed a 'lis' or 'lios' while a cashel can also be known as a 'caher' or 'cahir'. When such a site which was represented on an earlier map or maps has been removed and its construction material remains unknown, it is referred to here as an enclosure. Similarly the term enclosure will be used (i) where the construction is not typical of any rath or cashel, as at Cloonagh (223) where large orthostats form part of the edge and (ii) where associated monuments suggest that the monument pre-dates ringforts, with examples at Killadangan (231) and at Knockfin (235). The term ringfort will be applied (i) where both stone and earth appear in roughly equal amounts in the enclosing element (as with most examples), and (ii) where the composition of the surviving bank could not be made out as at Kilsallagh Upper (212). Every cashel and rath belongs to an overall monument classification of fort or ringfort.

Local enquiries produced the probable site of the fort which gave Knockaraha its name (241), while Knox seems to suggest that Belclare Castle (263) was built on or close to the site of a fort when he states 'The castle of Belclare near the modern house, may be taken to have been the successor of the fort called Cruachan of Aigill; if it was not on the site of the Dun' (Knox 1908, 305). This also happens to satisfy the local folklore in circulation up until the 1970s that Belclare House Hotel would never prosper, as it was reputedly built on a ringfort.

The majority of these sites are located on high ground on the top or sides of hills, drumlins or ridges. As a result, we find a good number with most impressive, spectacular commanding views, in particular those in Bouris, Carrownalurgan, Durless, Knappaghmore and Knockfin.

Ringforts were constructed as permanent residences and were also used when necessary for the temporary housing of livestock. Farming was the mainstay in Early Christian Ireland, with animals kept principally for meat, milk and hides. The domestic house or houses of the occupiers took up but a small area of the fort interior – much of the remainder could be utilised for the keeping of animals, either nocturnally or during prolonged periods of inclement weather. Entrances to the forts as a general rule of thumb are away from the prevailing westerly winds, somewhere in the eastern half of these circular sites.

They are generally held to originate from the Early Christian period onwards, though excavation at a rath on the Swinford bypass in Co. Mayo obtained definite Iron Age dates (100–200 BC) from charcoal samples, recovered from internal house foundations (Walsh 1993). Up until the late 1980's, there had been only two other forts in County Mayo excavated, at Letterkeen Wood near Newport (O'Riordáin and MacDermott 1952) and at Ardcloon in Templemore parish (Rynne 1956). Some recent archaeological testing in conjunction with road widening was carried out near sites at Carrownalurgan (189) and Streamstown (238) but revealed nothing of antiquity at either location.

Altogether there are ninety-four monuments in this listing, which break down as forty-two cashels, thirteen raths, eighteen ringforts and twenty-one enclosures, many of which have been removed. Taking the group as a whole, nearly 60% are located between sea level and the 90m contour, with 26% between 90-122m, 5% from 122-152m and 2% from 213-244m. This preference for a siting between 90-122m is reflected in the cashel distribution where 31% are located.

Souterrains or stone-built underground rooms are also incorporated into this chapter. These are generally and reasonably believed to have been used as hiding places from attack, or as an underground storage area for perishable foods. They consist of a passage, which is usually narrow and which provides access through a small cubby hole or creep into a larger room called a chamber. Access can be difficult but, once inside, chambers are usually spacious enough in which to stand. Three sites in the main listing contain souterrains (148, 160 and 234), while a further two examples were found in isolation (244 and 245).

Plate 17b: Uniform circular univallate rath in Cloonmonad (194) from W.

CASHELS 146-187

146 Bellataleen
O.S. 87:11:4 (4604 2150)
Site 06301 OD 61-91

Here there is a univallate cashel with current internal diameters of 25m N-S by 33m E-W. Good internal and external facing stones can be made out at intervals; this is best between SE and SW where it reads 2.3m in original thickness, averages 0.7m high internally but only 0.2m high externally. A break 4m wide in ESE may mark part or all of the original entrance. Interior contains numerous features: (i) Hollow round **house site** 4.7m N-S by 6.3m E-W internally, located near the centre, (ii) another **house site** 5m across internally against the inner face of cashel wall in NE and (iii) tentative remains of a third sub-circular **house** some 5.5m in overall diameters. Later field wall cuts the site in two.

147 Boheh (E.D. Kilsallagh)
O.S. 96:8:2 (8315 4041)
Site 018 ✔ OD 91-122

A rather poorly preserved univallate cashel with present internal diameters of 23m N-S by 28m E-W. Generally enclosed by a collapsed wall spread 1.5m wide, while some original inner facing 0.5m high survives along S. There is an irregular hollow feature 6.5m across overall, near the centre. Another feature in NNW is the remains of a turf clamp base.

148 Brackloon
O.S. 87:16:6 (8749 0332)
Site 047 ✔ OD 91-122

Located on fairly high ground in Brackloon Wood, this bivallate cashel has present internal diameters of 25m across. Both the inner and outer walls survive as collapsed stone spreads, and there is no original facing in evidence. Between W and N the outer wall spread is clearest, and here an intervening fosse 2m wide is also best defined. The entrace 2m wide is located in W.

   Souterrain in SW sector is formed of two distinct elements. The first (i), a passage-cum-chamber, is aligned NE-SW for 9m and is now only roofed for 3m at SW end; it reaches 1.2m high and 1.5m wide internally and contains a small vent at roof level at SW end. A narrow creep on its SE wall provides access to (ii) the second chamber aligned E-W for 7.5m; this reaches 1.8m high and 2.55m wide internally and contains a well-built alcove in the E wall. The construction method practised was trenching followed by corbelled building, though some natural outcrop occurs at N and E wall of the second chamber.

149 Brackloon
O.S. 87:16:3 (8562 1463)
Site 08801 OD 61-91

Poorly preserved univallate cashel with present internal diameters of 25m N-S by 22m E-W. Enclosing stone spread is low internally while externally it varies from 0.7m to 1.2m high. Partly overgrown wall 1.1m thick and 0.3m high and of uncertain antiquity survives along S. Site interior is a little uneven and is said locally to contain a **children's burial ground** (269).

150 Carrowkeel
O.S. 87:6:5 (3772 3277)
Site 012 ✔ OD 0-30
Cahernaran

This overgrown univallate cashel has overall diameters at present of 30m N-S by 33m E-W. Occasional low facing stones survive while a broad stone spread (from 5m to 6m in SE and W) forms the enclosing element. No entrance or internal features discernible, this cashel is just above the high water tide level.

151 Carrowkeel
O.S. 87:10:3 (3971 2843)
Site 013 ✔ OD 0-30

Nearly circular univallate cashel with original internal diameters of 24m. Some low inner facing at intervals with a later wall built on part of the edge. Later used as a tree-ring enclosure as attested to by the presence of mature sycamore and beech on the perimeter.

152 Carrowmore
O.S. 98:9:1 (0420 2445)
Site 013 ✔ OD 91-122

Circular univallate cashel 28m across internally at present and with a later wall on its edge. Original stone bank averages 3m wide and 0.7m high. Original outer facing stones 0.3 to 0.5m high survive at intervals but no inner facing evident. Part of an associated adjacent fence to E.

153 Cartoor
O.S. 96:4:4 (7490 4986)
Site 008 ✔ OD 30-61
Plate 25b

Almost circular univallate cashel with a foundation bank of earth and stone nearly 3m wide throughout; this bank averages 0.5m high but reaches 1.3m externally between SE and NW. Internal diameters from the edge of this bank measure 24m. Original outer facing is best evidenced externally reaching 0.7m along S. No clear inner facing. Tentative traces of a circular area 8m across to NNW of centre is a possible hut site.

154 Cartoor
O.S. 96:8:2 (7905 4490)
Site 016 ✔ OD 30-61

Much collapsed univallate cashel with a later wall on its edge and with current internal diameters of 30m. The collapsed wall spread reads 2m wide in N and up to 5m wide along S; some low outer facing stones are built into this foundation bank (beneath cashel wall); bank varies externally from 0.9m high in N to 1.9m in W. Gap 1.2m wide in E seems late.

155 Cartoor
O.S. 96:4:4 (7415 5068)
Site 045 OD 30-61

Roughly circular univallate cashel with internal diameters at present of 20m N-S by 18m E-W. Generally enclosed by a low bank or scarp, yet good original facing up to 1.6m thick survives between N and E. This seldom reaches 0.2m high internally, but it is much better preserved on the exterior where it achieves two courses 0.7m high. Entrance 5m wide lies in W. Large amounts of rock outcrop just outside W and NW. Landowner names this the 'Tower Field'.

156 Cloonagh
O.S. 87:12:5 (7970 1820)
Site 051 OD 61-91

Poorly preserved oval-shaped bivallate cashel with present internal diameters of 18.5m N-S by 24m E-W. Both enclosing walls are in a ruinous state while a fosse 1.4m wide can only be made out between E and SE. Outer wall spread is only evident along SE and W. A later rectangular building was constructed on the inner and outer wall remains in SW. The drop from the inner wall to the outer ground level along N is 3.3m. Interior is flat and featureless.

157 Cloonagh
O.S. 87:12:5 (7882 1776)
Site 093 OD 61-91

Poorly preserved univallate cashel with diameters at present of 13m N-S by 17m E-W internally and 19m N-S by 24.5m E-W overall. Enclosed by a collapsed wall 4.3m wide at most, with some inner facing reaching 0.4m high along W. A band of rubble in S probably hides some considerable original facing. Two **hut sites** are located in NE sector; one 3.2m N-S by 4m E-W internally is against the inner edge of the cashel wall, while the second one against its outer face is poorly preserved and 2.3m N-S internally. A conjoined sub-circular feature at the S is suggested at this cashel by a curving bank outside this sector.

158 Cuilleen
O.S. 96:4:2 (7960 5722)
Site 009 ✔ OD 30-61

Sub-circular remains of an overgrown univallate cashel. While no E-W diameter could be read, the current N-S diameter is 23m internally. Enclosing bank of stone and earth varies from 1.7m to 2.6m wide, 0.2m to 0.7m in internal height and 0.7m to 1m in external height. Some original outer facing 0.5m high survives between N and E. A gap 5.5m wide in E may be the entrance. There is a more recent wall on the edge of the site today.

159 Cuilleen
O.S. 86:16:6 (9150 0622)
Site 020 OD 213-244

On a flat terrace on SW slopes of Ben Goram. Oval-shaped univallate cashel whose enclosing bank is irregular along S for some distance. The bank is mostly of stone mixed with earth and forming outer walling along E and SE. It averages 2.5m wide and reaches 1m high at most both internally and externally. Original wall thickness of 1.5m was read in NNE. Gap 2m wide in N seems original. Outer fosse 2m wide at most runs outside NE to SW. Interior contains two small **huts**; one near centre measures 2.2m N-S by 3.9m E-W, while the second one 2.2m internally lies against the inner edge of the site in NE. Both stand 0.25m high. Present internal diameters 38m N-S by 27m E-W.

160 Durless
O.S. 96:8:3 (9000 4215)
Site 019 ✔ OD 61-91
Fig. 15

Nearly circular univallate cashel with a later wall on top and current internal diameters of 20m. Construction where visible is of small irregular schist flags. Both inner and outer facing 0.5m high at most is in evidence, most notably at N and WSW where an original wall thickness of 1.8m can be read. A slight berm 2m wide and 0.5m high runs outside W to N sector. **Souterrain** in NW interior is 7.3m NNE-SSW and extends beneath and outside the cashel wall. It reaches 1.6m high and 1.9m wide at most and is roofed by nine large lintels. Near its SSW end is a small rectangular embrasure.

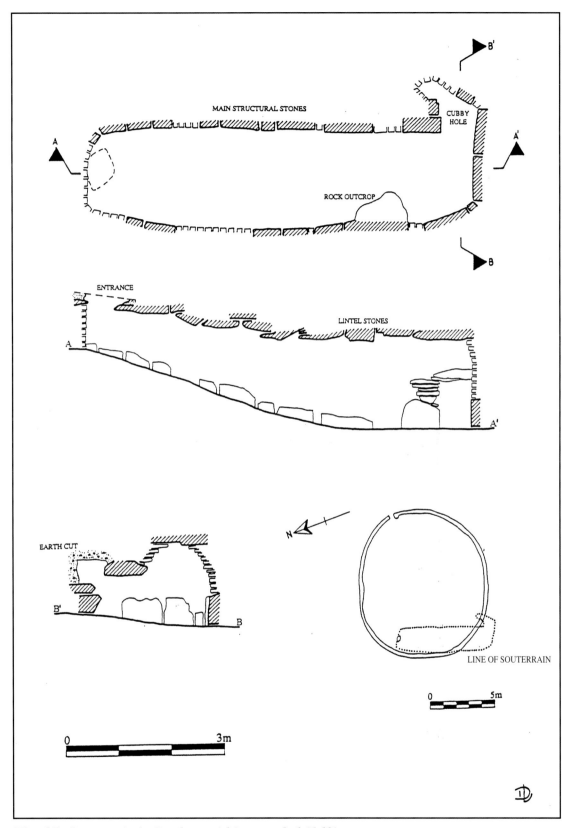

Fig. 15: Souterrain in Durless within a cashel (160).

161 Durless
O.S. 96:8:3 (8900 4052)
Site 02001 ✔ OD 61-91

Fairly circular univallate cashel with current internal diameters of 22m N-S by 20m E-W. Enclosed by a stony bank 1m high internally at most (NE to S) and reaching 0.8m high externally along N. This bank averages 2m wide but this is increased considerably at ESE. Some low inner facing occurs, mostly in the eastern half, while outer facing 0.35m high along W gives an original cashel wall thickness of 1.2m. A berm 2m wide and 0.8m high surrounds most of the site while a recent wall today encloses the cashel. Interior contains an unusual small circular hollow in NW.

162 Fahburen
O.S. 87:11:6 (6449 1963)
Site 119 OD 30-61

Roughly circular univallate cashel with internal diameters at present of 23m N-S by 20m E-W. Bordered by a collapsed wall from 4m to 6m wide at the base with no original facing evident. It contains a small **hut** 4.3m N-S by 3.8m E-W internally in the SSW sector. Some large cairns within the interior appear to be the result of clearance.

163 Glenbaun
O.S. 97:1:1 (0480 5580)
Site 00101 ✔ OD 152-183

A much collapsed univallate cashel with original internal diameters of 32m N-S by 30m E-W. The collapsed wall averages 2 to 3m wide but reaches as much as 6.5m along S and from W to N. All along NW it is tallest at 1.6m high externally. Original inner facing 0.35m high is evident near E and S while a substantial cashel wall of small flat stones reaches 0.6m high internally near W. Original outer walling, where it occurs, is much lower but does give a cashel wall thickness of 1.2m in SSW. One stone aligned NW-SE on bank in SE may mark one side of an entrance. A **hut** 1.6m across internally lies within the cashel wall spread at S, with a further possible hut in N interior. Outline of a fosse 2.3m wide and 0.6m deep at most outside W to S sector. Hint of a second enclosing wall outside E, and W to N sector.

164 Glencally
O.S. 97:1:2 (0840 5440)
Site 00201 ✔ OD 152-183

Almost circular univallate cashel with present internal diameters of 20m. Some of the original inner and outer wall face reaches 0.4m high and gives a cashel wall 1.7m thick. Construction is of generally thin, flat flags. The base of the enclosing element consists primarily of a bank of stone and earth up to 4m wide, 0.5m high internally and 1.8m high externally at most. Gap 1.2m wide in ESE is probably original, with a stony bank lining its N side externally. A later field wall on the edge forms a sheep pen outside S sector.

165 Glencally
O.S. 97:1:4 (0340 4650)
Site 003 ✔ OD 61-91

Present diameters of this univallate cashel read 20m internally and 25m overall. Original outer walling of large undressed schist reaches 1.1m high along NNE and E, while inner facing only reaches 0.2m high for a few metres. No original thickness reading was obtained. Cashel wall was incorporated into a bank of stone and earth 2.5m wide at most, rather low internally and up to 1.5m high externally. Part of the enclosing element is cut away in SE. Some rock outcrop in the interior and no clear entrance. Locally known as a caher.

166 Glencally
O.S. 97:1:1 (0610 5350)
Site 034 OD 91-122
Poorly preserved, fairly circular univallate cashel with internal diameters at present measuring 16m across. Uniformly enclosed by a low collapsed stony spread 3m wide at most, 0.5m high at most internally and reaching 1.4m high externally. Site interior contains a stone **hut** 3.3m across internally, in N sector. Seasonal flooding in the stream at SE has damaged the edge.

167 Glinsk
O.S. 97:8:3 (880 4020)
Site 007 ✔ OD 91-122
Collapsed univallate cashel with present internal diameters of 19m N-S by 17m E-W. Bordered by a bank of stone and earth from 2.7m to 4m wide, generally rather low internally but which drops 2.5m to outer ground level along N. Original inner facing 0.65m high at most is only visible from SSE to NW. Good outer facing reaching 0.75m high can be seen at intervals between ENE and SE, while a good stretch 0.5m high runs from SSE to SW. There is a natural ledge 3m wide and 1m high outside the E to S sector. Site interior has a 3m wide fosse just inside the SE to SW sector.

168 Killadangan
O.S. 87:7:6 (6792 3391)
Site 015 ✔ OD 0-15
On raised ground near the southern end of Annagh Island East and set on a small promontory. Small circular univallate cashel with present internal diameter of 11.7m. Enclosed by collapsed wall 2m wide on average but somewhat wider to ESE and NW. This wall is low internally while it reaches its greatest external height of between 2m and 2.6m from S to NW. An artificial ledge 1m wide runs outside the SW sector.

169 Killadangan
O.S. 87:11:3 (6424 2601)
Site 032 ✔ OD 0-30
Poorly defined circular univallate cashel with internal diameter at present of 19m. Generally enclosed by a bank of stone and earth, now in a rather ruinous state; this bank averages 0.9m wide and seldom exceeds 0.3m high. However, with the natural slope in outer ground level, it drops by as much as 1.3m along W reaching 3m or a little more along N. A line of sturdy outer facing stones 0.6m high survive between NW and NNW. Site interior contains a large concrete water tank in NE but is otherwise overgrown.

170 Killadangan
O.S. 87:11:3 (6505 2406)
Site 033 ✔ OD 0-30
Poorly preserved univallate cashel with present internal diameters of 21m N-S by 18.5m E-W. No original facing in evidence, rather it is enclosed by a collapsed spread 3.5m wide at most; this wall averages 0.7m high internally (reaches 1.2m from S to W) and 1.1m high externally. Extra thickness to cashel wall spread in SE accommodates a **hut** 2.5m across internally.

171 Killadangan
O.S. 87:12:1 (6802 2437)
Site 03501 ✔ OD 0-30

Circular univallate cashel with internal diameters of 18m at present. For most of its circumference, the collapsed cashel wall is in a poor state averaging 2m wide and from 0.2m to 0.5m high, though it reaches 1m to 1.5m high externally between S and W. Along ESE however some inner and outer facing 0.35m high gives a wall thickness of 1.3m. Large amounts of sea shells are incorporated into the bank at the base of the cashel wall (2), along S. Gap of 3m in N is the likeliest entrance.

172 Killeencoff
O.S. 88:9:5 (0090 1890)
Site 04801 ✔ OD 91-122

Poorly preserved univallate cashel enclosed by a spread of stones 1.5m wide on average; its internal height never exceeds 0.5m while it reaches 1.2m high externally in NNW. There is no original cashel wall construction in evidence. Present internal diameters both read 21m. A number of orthostats in the interior are part of a later field wall which ran through the cashel. There is a tentative annex 8m long N-S by 6m wide against the NE sector externally.

173 Kilsallagh Lower
O.S. 86:12:5 (8160 1995)
Site 00901 ✔ OD 0-30

On a low knoll just above the sea shore. Nearly circular univallate cashel, in a rather poor condition, with a more recent field wall on a collapsed wall spread 2m wide on average. Only in SSW beside a cattle gap can any original facing be seen; this reads only 0.25m high externally. Widening of the Louisburgh-Westport road has damaged the edge between WNW and N, and the drop to outer ground level is steepest along here. Internal diameters today measure 23m.

174 Kilsallagh Upper
O.S. 86:16:4 (7590 0705)
Site 007 OD 91-122

This nearly circular univallate cashel lies on top of a drumlin with exceptionally scenic and strategic views all around. Enclosed mainly by a bank of stone and earth 2.5m wide and from 0.25m to 0.6m high, though reaching 1.2m high externally in W. Some inner facing 0.42m high survives along E, while between S and W original outer walling, three courses high, reaches 0.6m; smaller packing stones were used in the construction along here. Internal diameters at present read 24m. Interior contains two hummocks to N of centre.

175 Knappaghbeg
O.S. 88:16:1 (7590 0720)
Site 059 ✔ OD 91-122

Oval-shaped univallate cashel with current internal diameters of 25m N-S by 30m E-W. Enclosed by a bank of stone and earth 2.4m wide at most and from 0.7m to 1.5m high, with a more recent wall in some sectors. Outer facing stones 0.6m high survive at SSE while some outer walling 1m high (of rough undressed stones) can be found at SE and S. Interior contains a stone-lined **hut** 0.4m high in W sector; this measures 4.2m N-S by 5.4m E-W internally.

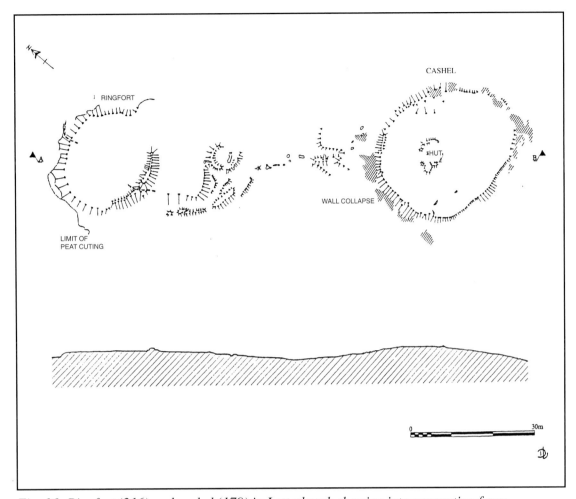

Fig. 16: Ringfort (216) and cashel (179) in Letterbrock showing interconnecting fence.

176 Knappaghmore
O.S. 98:1:1 (0570 6000)
Site 001 ✔ OD 122-152
See cover photograph
An almost circular univallate cashel with original internal diameter of 30m. Its enclosing wall of irregular flat slabs and blocks survives practically throughout, with an original wall thickness of 1.5m. It reaches a maximum internal height of 1.7m near S while elsewhere internally it varies from 1m to 1.5m high. Externally its height varies little between 1.5m and 2m. Beneath the wall is a stony bank 3m wide on average and 1m high at most – this bank is most noticeable in S half. Small internal hummocks indicate possible features while a vegetation band 12 by 8m in NW may represent a contemporary structure or feature within the cashel.

177 Knappaghmore
O.S. 88:13:5 (0830 0160)
Site 056 ✔ OD 122-152
In the same wooded setting as the last cashel, this univallate example has original internal diameters of 18.5m N-S by 20.5m E-W. Construction is of irregular blocks and flags with larger ones used near the base. Inner face of the cashel wall varies from 1m to 1.5m high but reaches 1.9m high along N. Outer facing, varying from 0.4m to 1m high, gives a cashel wall thickness of 2.5m at most. Beneath the wall, a stony bank 0.8m high and 1.5m wide can be seen internally between E and NNW. A stony area 5m by 3m and 1m high, in NW, probably demarcates a **hut** site.

178 Lanmore
O.S. 98:5:5 (1400 3494)
Site 008 ✔ OD 91-122

Poorly preserved univallate cashel whose collapsed wall was constructed on a bank of stone and earth; this bank is only visible internally along E where it reaches 0.45m high, while externally it reaches 1m high along N. Inner facing reaches 0.3m high and survives in E and S. Outer wall face is evident at 0.8m high along E and S and reaches 1.2m high in SW. An original wall thickness of 1.3m was read in S. Entrance gap 3m wide in NNW. Present internal diameters of 27m N-S by 24m E-W.

179 Letterbrock
O.S. 97:8:5 (7870 3480)
Site 008 ✔ OD 91-122
Fig. 16

Generally enclosed by a stony spread from 1.6m to 3.2m wide, this univallate cashel has internal diameters at present of 25m N-S by 31m E-W. The enclosing element takes the form of an earthen bank in NW. While the wall spread is low internally, it reaches 0.9m high externally. A 2m wide spread of stone runs parallel to the cashel wall outside WSW to NW, while a fosse 1m wide and 0.3m deep runs inside the NW to NNE sector. Interior contains an irregular stone structure like a hut with overall dimensions of 6.5m NE-SW by 5m NW-SE. Associated fence of earth and stone runs NW-SE to connect with a nearby ringfort (216).

180 Letterbrock
O.S. 97:8:5 (8040 3350)
Site 025 OD 91-122

A simple univallate cashel cut in two by a later road. Internal diameters at present read 22m NNW-SSE by 26m ENE-WSW. Best defined in E half where a stony bank 2m to 3m wide and 0.5m high internally encloses it. No clear inner facing, while good facing 0.4m to 0.7m high on the outside is most evident between E and S.

181 Liscarney
O.S. 98:5:2 (0910 4040)
Site 021 ✔ OD 91-122

Poorly preserved univallate cashel with a spring well outside NNE feeding a streamlet through the interior. Enclosed mainly by collapsed stone spread from 2.2m to 5m wide, which reaches 0.5m high at most. One low outer facing stone 0.2m high in S. Interior is very damp, and diameters at present read 19m N-S by 22m E-W internally and 23m N-S by 27m E-W overall.

182 Moyhastin
O.S. 88:10:1 (2950 2555)
Site 049 ✔ OD 61-91

This overgrown univallate cashel stands in a good commanding location. Only one diameter could be read, and that 33m NW-SE internally. Enclosed by a broad spread of stones from 4m to 6m wide generally. Some low rough walling is visible here and there, but no original wall thickness. Wall spread averages 0.5m high internally though it reaches 1.3m along NW, while externally it is generally higher, reaching 1.7m along E. Blackthorn chokes interior and much of the edge.

183 Moyhastin
O.S. 88:10:2 (3155 2802)
Site 050 ✔ OD 61-91
Overgrown univallate cashel with occasional outer facing 0.3m high, best evidenced between N and SE. Low inner facing along E gives a wall thickness of 1.2m. Most of W sector of fort is overgrown and rubble covers much of the edge here also. A rough N-S internal diameter reads 30m.

184 Oughty
O.S. 97:11:4 (5340 1830)
Site 030 OD 152-183
This bivallate cashel with current internal diameters of 24m is enclosed internally by a broad bank of stone and earth 4m wide at most. Sections of the original inner cashel wall from 1.3m (W) to 1.7m (N) thick are built on this bank. Inner facing 0.5m high forms an almost continuous line from NNW to SE, while outer facing is scarcer and lower. Intervening fosse 1.5m wide at the base and 0.85m deep externally is only clearly in evidence from SE to SSW. Gap 1.5m wide in inner bank in SE has a corresponding causeway over the fosse. The outer wall in the form of a 1.6m wide spread of stones, 0.6m high on average, is only visible along SSE. Interior contains a **hut** 6.5m N-S by 7.5m E-W (internally), to S of centre. Much of the W parts of this cashel have been damaged.

185 Owenwee
O.S. 97:4:4 (6810 4640)
Site 021 ✔ OD 91-122
This small irregularly shaped univallate cashel has internal diameter readings of 15m N-S by 11.5m E-W at present. A modern enclosing wall is built on the 1m spread of the original cashel wall. Some large original outer facing blocks, as much as 1m high, survive at intervals. Gap in WNW is modern.

186 Pollanoughty
O.S. 97:10:6 (4100 2100)
Site 00901 ✔ OD 152-183
Here, a univallate cashel has its enclosing wall formed of a collection of large and small undressed stones and flags, packed together with earth to form a bank; this bank stands anything from 0.4m to 1.1m higher than the outer ground level. Original inner walling 0.7m high at most survives best from N to SSW, while outer walling is visible in most sectors reaching 0.6m high in SW. An original wall thickness varies from 2.5m to 3m. A natural vertical rock face 1.5m high lies just outside SSE to SSW, while site interior contains a sheep pen.

187 Pollanoughty
O.S. 97:10:6 (4060 2080)
Site 010 ✔ OD 152-183
Within 70m of the last site, this univallate cashel has present internal diameters of 25.5m. The original cashel wall had a later wall superimposed on it, but both are now badly damaged. Internal facing, while never exceeding 0.2m high, survives from N to SW while outer facing 0.35m high at most is best in SSE and along S to WSW. The original cashel wall reads 2.3m thick at SW. A stone spread 6m N-S by 9m E-W in the interior represents a possbile hut site.

* * *

RATHS 188-200

Raths are circular, or nearly circular areas enclosed by a bank or banks in which earth is the most dominant component. Gravel, daub and even shell have been found mixed through the earth at various sites. The construction of the bank sometimes, but not always, results in the creation of a trench or drain, referred to as a fosse. Over the centuries many fosses have become silted up and may only be detected through excavation. Of the total, the most labour-intensive from a construction point of view would appear to be those at Carrownalurgan (189, 190), Clerhaun (192) and Rossbeg (200).

188 Bellataleen
O.S. 87:11:4 (4604 1867)
Site 080 OD 91-122
Fig. 17 + Plate 11b
Consists of the S half of a univallate rath with an E-W internal diameter of 27m. Enclosing bank is formed of earth, gravel and stone and reads 3.4m wide at most; it is extremely low internally and from 0.7m to 1.4m high externally. An outer fosse 1m wide and 0.5m deep at most is clearest between S and W. Interior contains a low rectangular outline of earth 2m N-S by 4m E-W overall, while a possible collapsed **souterrain** is suggested to S of centre; here a bleached vegetation band delimits a passage 4m long NNE-SSW with a chamber 2m across at its S end.

189 Carrownalurgan
O.S. 88:5:4 (0482 3611)
Site 083 ✔ OD 30-61
This is a classic univallate rath whose broad enclosing bank of earth and stone varies from 5m to 7.3m wide at the base. It reaches its maximum internal and external heights of 1.5m and 2.7m respectively with some stonework evident in the outer edge along NW. An outer fosse 4m wide and 0.4m deep at most can be seen in most sectors. A later wall outside SW gives the rath a bivallate appearance. Interior contains an inscribed limestone slab dated 1723. The Latin inscription in high relief translates "Pray for the soul of Peter Browne for whom this was carved". Crest-to-crest diameters measure 38m N-S by 35m E-W.

Plate 18: Inscribed 18th century slab in a rath at Carrownalurgan (189).

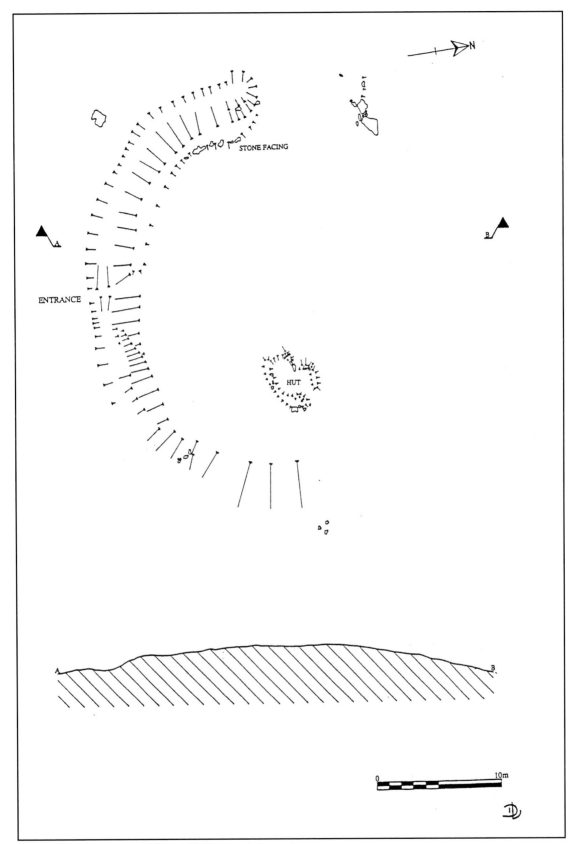

Fig. 17: Rath in Bellataleen (188) containing a hut.

190 Carrownalurgan
O.S. 88:5:4 (0690 3680)
Site 084 ✔ OD 30-61

Crest-to-crest diameters for this univallate rath both read 25m. Its broad enclosing bank averages 8m wide throughout, averages 1.2m high internally and from 1m to 1.5m high externally. Site interior appears hollow, and in S sector the outline of a **hut** 0.3m high and 3.7m across overall can be seen.

191 Carrowrevagh
O.S. 97:12:6 (8880 1920)
Site 016 ✔ OD 91-122

Univallate rath whose enclosing bank of earth is flush with the site interior. On the outside the scarp edge varies from 0.5 to 1m high and contains some stone facing along W. Poorly preserved fosse outside NW and SE while a 3m wide gap in W is the likeliest entrance. Diameters across the top measure 22m.

192 Clerhaun
O.S. 88:5:4 (0540 3060)
Site 069 ✔ OD 30-61

A bivallate rath with crest-to-crest diameters of 20m N-S by 24.5m E-W and whose banks are composed of earth and gravel. The inner enclosing bank is flush with the interior, while it varies from 1.4m (N to E) to 2.5m (NNW) high externally. Intervening fosse 2.2m wide on average can only be seen in the western half – a causeway effect in WNW hints at the original entrance here. Outer bank contains more stone than its inner counterpart, averages 1.5m to 2m wide, 0.3m to 0.7m high internally while it reaches 1m high externally at most.

193 Cloonmonad
O.S. 88:5:1 (0630 4380)
Site 029 ✔ OD 0-30

Partly damaged univallate rath in the middle of Springfield housing estate. Enclosing bank is mainly earthen and, while very low internally, varies from 1.2m to 1.8m high externally. The enclosing element and part of the interior have been cut away between NE and S. Foundations of a later building can be seen against its SW exterior. Diameter across the top measures 35m NNE-SSW.

194 Cloonmonad
O.S. 88:5:2 (0900 4030)
Site 031 ✔ OD 0-30
Plate 17b

Univallate rath with diameters across the top of 34m N-S by 32m E-W. Bank of earth is level with the site interior while externally it varies between 0.4m to 0.8m high. Entrance 4.7m wide in SW has a corresponding causeway over the fosse. Fosse averages 1.3m wide and is 0.45m deep at most. Interior contains an oval depression 0.55m deep measuring 3.6m N-S by 4.3m E-W in SSW, with a smaller hollow in SE. In a rather low-lying location with former marshy ground to S.

195 Glaspatrick
O.S. 87:9:3 (2155 2461)
Site 027 ✔ OD 0-30

A much overgrown univallate rath with an E-W internal diameter of 20m. Only visible at intervals, the bank was constructed of earth, though a little stone facing is evident – bank averages 3m wide and while it reaches 1m high externally in E, it appears to be much lower internally throughout.

196 Glaspatrick
O.S. 87:10:1 (2978 2499)
Site 030 ✔ OD 0-30

As with one in Bellataleen (188), this consists of the S half of a univallate rath with E-W internal diameter of 17m. Enclosing bank of earth only averages 1m wide overall and 0.6m high internally and externally. The fosse in S half shows up as a band of rushes 2.6m wide and somewhat narrower between NW and E. A 5m wide area near NW possibly represents part of the entrance. Site interior has split levels with the N end 1.5m lower, and it contains a later rectangular building.

197 Kilsallagh Lower
O.S. 86:12:5 (8210 1505)
Site 025 ✔ OD 61-91

Fine univallate rath with internal diameters of 22.5m. Enclosing bank of earth is faced with stone along S and generally averages 4m wide at the base. Best preserved from E to SW where it reaches 0.6m high internally and from 0.8m to 1.2m high externally; the bank is level with the site interior elsewhere. A flat-bottomed fosse 2.5 to 4.2m wide and from 0.15m to 1m deep has an entrance causeway 3m wide at E. Against the bank in NNE, a circular area 0.45m high and 3.2m across is an associated **house**.

198 Knappaghmore
O.S. 88:13:1 (0150 0780)
Site 054 ✔ OD 30-61

Fairly circular univallate rath with rough internal diameters of 32m. Enclosing bank of earth and some stone reaches 5m in overall width. It is best preserved along S to NE at 2m high externally and 0.5m high internally; elsewhere it is rather low internally, though retaining a considerable height externally. Flat natural platform outside the bank in SSW to NW sectors. No trace of original entrance.

199 Oughty
O.S. 97:11:5 (6030 1600)
Site 053 OD 122-152

Another poorly preserved univallate rath, this time oval-shaped. Enclosing bank is built mostly of earth and survives best between E and S, where it reads 3.4m wide, up to 1m high internally and up to 2m high externally; elsewhere it is lowered internally while later walls obscure much of its outer edge. Interior is partly rocky with a split level of 1m. Rough diameters crest-to-crest read 28m.

200 Rossbeg
O.S. 87:8:3 (8942 3880)
Site 021 ✔ OD 30-61

Strategically and impressively situated on a drumlin, the earthen bank of this univallate rath has been levelled internally throughout; this scarp varies from 0.8m high to 2.8m along S to SW. A diminution to the scarp for 8m in SE probably represents part of the entrance. Some elongated trenches inside and parallel to the bank in western half are curious. It seems likely they represent a collapsed souterrain and they average 1.8m wide and 0.7m deep. A small hut 2.5m across internally and 0.3m high lies NW of centre. Diameters across the top measure 30m.

This fort, according to local tradition, is the original stronghold of the O'Malley tribe, of whom the famous Grace O'Malley was a descendant.

* * *

RINGFORTS 201-218

Both cashels and raths, as previously indicated, belong to a family of monuments usually referred to as ringforts. However where such monuments occur and there is uncertainty as to whether earth or stone is the most dominant component in the enclosing element, then the general term of ringfort will be applied. Any ringfort from the list below may be, or have been, a cashel or a rath. It is reasonable to assume that ringforts in areas of rock outcrop may have been cashels, as at Letterbrock (216), while those in more fertile earthen surroundings may have consisted of raths, with examples at Carrowmore (205) and Leckanvey (214).

201 Ardoley
O.S. 88:9:1 (0010 1700)
Site 047 OD 30-60
Circular univallate ringfort 22m across internally, located on N slope of a drumlin. Enclosing bank 2.8 to 3.5m wide is composed of stone, earth and gravel and is heavily overgrown; it reaches 0.9m high internally in N and S and 1m high externally along NNW. No clear entrance is visible, while interior is level.

202 Bellataleen
O.S. 87:10:6 (4560 1740)
Site 058 OD 122-152
Fig. 18
This univallate ringfort is bounded by a loose rudimentary wall spread 1m to 1.4m wide, with white quartz incorporated into many of the enclosing stones. It reaches 0.6m high internally, but is much lower internally and externally and rather poorly defined from W to SE. Interior contains a well faced stone **hut** 10m N-S by 11m E-W internally, in the NNE sector. This monument is located beneath cut-away bog.

203 Boheh (E.D. Kilsallagh)
O.S. 96:4:5 (8270 4646)
Site 017 ✔ OD 61-91
Internal diameters for this univallate ringfort both read 17.5m Its enclosing bank of earth and stone varies from 1.7m to 2.4m wide at the base, and the stone takes the form of facing 0.5m high internally at intervals. The bank is highest internally at 0.8m in the northern half and externally at 1.3m between E and NW. Only likely entrance is a lowering to the bank in E.

204 Carrowbaun
O.S. 88:5:6 (2160 3000)
Site 106 OD 61-91
Oval-shaped univallate ringfort with internal diameters of 19m N-S by 29m E-W. Enclosed by a bank of stone and earth which is reduced to a 0.4m high scarp in the northern half. Elsewhere, it averages 3m to 4m wide, 0.4m high internally and 0.8m high externally. No clear entrance but bank is lowest in ESE. A thickening to the enclosing bank in SE suggests an internal structure 5m across. Interior contains a glacial erratic.

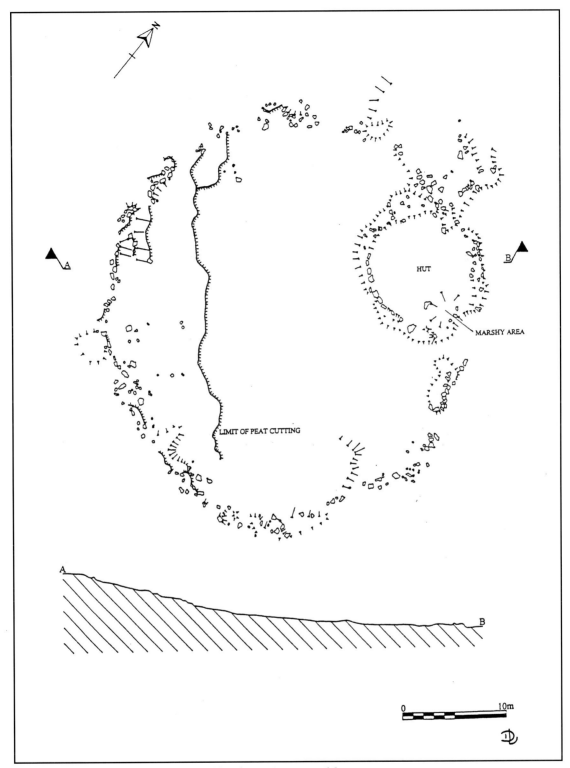

Fig. 18: Ringfort in Bellataleen (202) showing internal hut.

205 Carrowmore
O.S. 98:9:1 (0360 2490)
Site 02301 ✔ OD 91-122
Poorly preserved univallate ringfort with rough internal diameters of 18m N-S by 22m E-W. Site is cut by a later wall, and only the E half can be clearly made out. The much levelled bank reads 6m wide and varies in height from 0.6m internally to 0.9m externally.

206 Cartoor
O.S. 96:4:4 (7424 4975)
Site 043 OD 30-61

Small univallate ringfort with internal diameters of 17m whose enclosing bank is built of earth mostly, with stone supplementing it. The bank averages 2.3m wide throughout and is generally lower internally, though it does reach 0.8m high. Where it is lowest internally, it is highest externally reaching 1.2m along S – elsewhere externally it averages 0.9m high.

207 Cloghan
O.S. 88:5:4 (0210 3440)
Site 085 ✔ OD 30-61

This univallate ringfort shows evidence of a vague D-shaped annex outside its NE sector. Enclosing bank of stone and earth 2.8m wide is best preserved along N to E and in W, averaging 0.5m high. In most other sectors, it is reduced to a scarp from 0.9m to 1.9m high – some outer stone facing in NNE. Outside N to SE and from S to W runs a flat berm 3m wide and 0.7m high. The only gap is a 3.7m wide break in WNW. Internal diameters read 26m.

208 Cuilleen
O.S. 96:4:3 (9205 6020)
Site 010 OD 152-183
Plate 25a

Bivallate ringfort whose outer bank and fosse are only evident along SW. The fosse averages 2.5m wide and 0.5m deep, while the outer bank is most tentative yet present. Inner bank from 3m to 6m wide is of earth and stone, with the stone taking the form of facing; this bank is flush with the outer ground level in the northern half while it varies from 0.6m to 1.4m high internally throughout. Site interior is uneven, with a **hut** 7.3m across overall in the SW sector. Current diameters read 30m overall by about 20m internally.

209 Glaspatrick
O.S. 87:10:1 (2902 2581)
Site 029 ✔ OD 0-30

Heavily choked with blackthorns and briars, only part of the enclosing element could be accessed and that in the S and SW. Enclosing bank constructed of earth and stone, about 3m wide, 0.4m high internally and 1m high externally.

210 Glencally
O.S. 97:1:4 (0570 4750)
Site 004 ✔ OD 61-91

Oval-shaped univallate ringfort with present internal diameters of 17m N-S by 23m E-W. Enclosing bank is composed of earth and gravel but stone is most dominant, though no actual facing is present. It is best preserved from W to N 3.2m wide, and 1.2m high internally and externally. The drop from the bank top to the outer ground level is greatest along S at 3.5m. Gap of 2m in E is the likely entrance. This fort is referred to locally as a lis.

211 Killaghoor
O.S. 88:6:1 (2420 3810)
Site 110 OD 61-91

Nearly circular univallate ringfort whose bank of earth and stone has been reduced to a scarp throughout. Diameters across the top measure 15.7m. Height of scarp varies from 0.4m to 1.2m while it is absent along E. Slight circular hollow 1.6m across and 0.35m deep suggests part of a souterrain in the interior.

212 Kilsallagh Upper
O.S. 86:16:2 (7820 0810)
Site 008 ✔ OD 91-122
Fig. 19

Nearly circular trivallate ringfort with both internal diameters of 21m. Banks are heather-covered and composition could not be made out. Inner bank is broad, 3m to 4m wide and generally flat-topped at 1m wide; it averages 0.5m high internally and 1.3m high externally. Damp, flat fosse outside this is 2m to 3m wide and 1m deep externally at most. Both the intervening and outer banks are low, average 2m to 4m in width, but do not survive throughout. This site commands extensive views over much of Clew Bay.

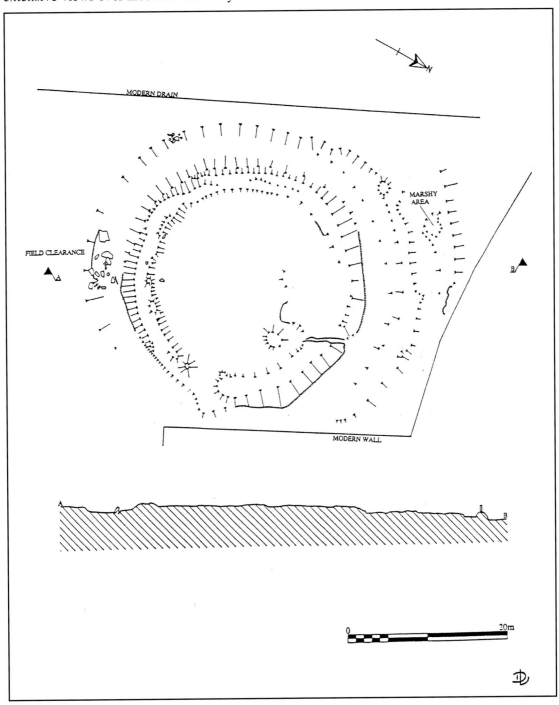

Fig. 19: Three-banked ringfort in Kilsallagh Upper (212).

213 Knappaghbeg
O.S. 88:14:1 (2650 0990)
Site 112 ✔ OD 30-61

Poorly defined sub-circular enclosure with internal diameters of 40m N-S by 34m E-W. Its bank of earth and stone 2.6m wide and 0.4m high is best preserved at S. Interior contains a pronounced, flat-topped mound 9.5m NW-SE by 6.5m wide and up to 2.5m high. Older residents refer to this place as 'cregganalisheen' while others call it a fort.

214 Leckanvey
O.S. 87:9:4 (0163 2185)
Site 025 ✔ OD 0-30

Very poorly preserved, partly overgrown bivallate ringfort. Much of the western half and part of the S have been cut away. Inner bank in the form of a scarp 2m high at least survives from NNE to E and from S to W – its outer slopes are formed of earth and stone. A fosse some 2m wide runs outside E sector, while the overgrown outer bank also survives as a scarp from 1.6m high along NE to 0.6m high near E. No diameters possible.

215 Leckanvey
O.S. 87:9:4 (0540 1870)
Site 026 OD 61-91

Situated on the top of a pronounced natural drumlin similar to that named Sheeroe elsewhere in the text (17) though not as pronounced. Named as Cahir Gall on Balds 1838 map. Poorly preserved univallate ringfort with internal diameters at present of 17m. Enclosed by a very low, overgrown bank of earth and stone with no trace of an entrance. Bank is practically reduced to a scarp 0.3m to 0.6m high throughout and site interior is level and featureless.

216 Letterbrock
O.S. 97:8:5 (6930 3590)
Site 028 OD 91-122
Fig. 16

Within 25m of a cashel (179) is this univallate ringfort with internal diameters of 19m. Bank is composed of medium and small stones mixed with gravel and best preserved from ESE to SSW – here it averages 3.9m wide, 1.3m high internally and externally, and flat-topped at 1m wide. In all other sectors it is reduced to a scarp. Traces of a fosse 2m wide and 0.2m deep outside the best preserved section of bank. Bank connecting this site to cashel (179) contains a small sub-circular stone structure of some antiquity, probably a hut site.

217 Letterbrock
O.S. 97:12:4 (7410 2210)
Site 058 ✔ OD 91-122

This univallate ringfort 16m N-S by 20m E-W internally is in the E sector of a large, roughly circular modern field. Bank is composed of stone and earth and reaches 6m in width. Occasional inner and outer facing stones occur, while the bank never exceeds 0.7m high internally and 1.5m high externally. An orthostat (56) stands 14m from outside of NNE edge.

218 Oughty
O.S. 97:15:1 (5470 1080)
Site 042 OD 91-122

Poor remains of a univallate ringfort whose enclosing bank of earth and stone is best preserved from WNW to N, where it averages 2.4m wide, from 0.2 to 0.9m high internally and 1m high externally. Along S to SW it survives as a scarp yet elsewhere the site edge is rather tentative. Rough internal diameters measure 20m. When the enclosing bank was damaged a number of years ago, a bullaun stone (260) was moved to the N closer to the road.

ENCLOSURES 219-239

It is likely that some of the monuments in this list also consisted of ringforts; such sites were represented on earlier O.S. maps. Today, however, no physical evidence of the site or its enclosing element can be identified on the ground surface, and as a result the term enclosure will have to suffice. Antiquities located at Cloonmonad (224), Drumminaweelaun (227), Killeencoff (233), Knappaghmanagh (234) and Streamstown (238) may have originally been ringforts. Other enclosures which today resemble ringforts have not been classified as such because of their association with structures or features which suggest they are of greater antiquity than ringforts, e.g. Killadangan (231) and Knockfin (235). Most of the other enclosures here cannot be more accurately classified due either to the irregularity of their plan (220), insufficient remains (221) or the unusual construction technique used (223).

219 Carrowkeel
O.S. 87:10:3 (4230 2760)
Site 067 OD 0-30
Small, oval-shaped univallate enclosure with overall diameters of 6.5m N-S by 10m E-W. Enclosing bank is mainly earthen, about 2m wide and from 0.4m to 1m high. Interior is hollow in appearance and featureless.

220 Carrowmacloughlin, Glencally, Teevenacroaghy
O.S. 87:13:6 (2090 0180)
Site 04301 ✔ OD 610-671
Plate 4
Surrounding three cairns (21), this irregular-shaped area 75m N-S by 82m E-W may have served as a prehistoric enclosure. Used in more modern times as part of the pilgrimage 'turas', a trackway 2m wide forms its edge in most sectors. The name 𝕽𝖊𝖎𝖑𝖎𝖌 𝕸𝖍𝖚𝖎𝖗𝖊 at this site is generally assumed to refer to the cairns, but it could be a name used for the entire site. Interestingly, locals refer to the enclosed area as the 'garraí mór'.

221 Carromacloughlin
O.S. 87:9:5 (0290 2200)
Site 094 OD 30-61
Traces of a univallate enclosure with a curving bank of stone and earth survive only along E sector. The bank varies from 0.2m to 0.7m high and averages 2.7m wide at the base. Cut by a N-S wall with no trace to the W. Located in the lower part of a valley.

222 Cloonagh
O.S. 87:12:5 (8060 1860)
Site 041 ✔ OD 30-61
Near the centre of the townland, this rather circular outline on the 1838 O.S. map cannot be identified on the ground surface today. Its removal probably preceded 1901, as evidenced by its omission from the 6″ O.S. map of that year.

223 Cloonagh
O.S. 87:12:5 (8035 1930)
Site 092 ✔ OD 30-61
Fig. 20

A small, stone-lined enclosure 10m N-S by 13.5m E-W internally. It is enclosed by a group of ten large orthostats 1.2m high at most, all interconnected by a later wall. Gap 0.7m wide in WSW is the only entrance. Interior contains one tall sheet of rock outcrop. Classification as a stone circle cannot be dismissed for while no clear portal or recumbent stones are evident, the plan resembles that at Drombeg, Co. Cork, in size and morphology (Waddell 1998, 170).

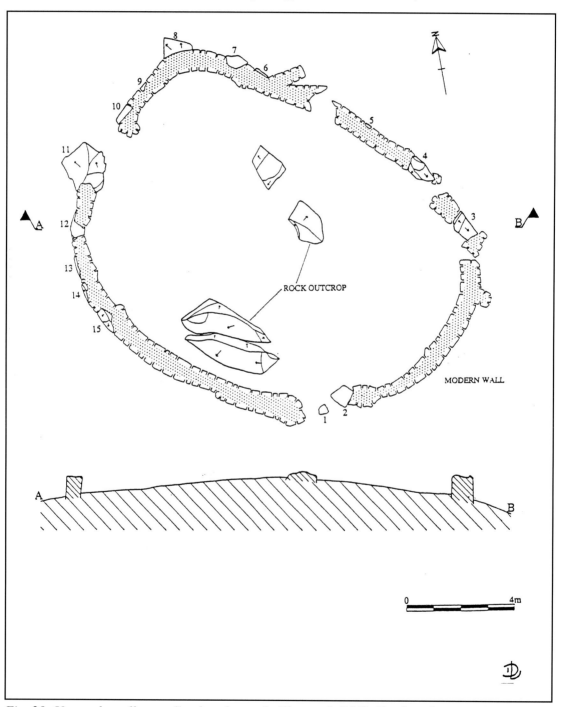

Fig. 20: Unusual small stone-lined enclosure in Cloonagh (223). Numbered stones show orthostats.

224 Cloonmonad
O.S. 88:5:1 (0350 4470)
Site 028 ✔ OD 0-30
There are no surface remains of this site to be seen today. Roughly circular on the 1838 map, the 1929 edition shows the 100 foot contour delimiting much of its edge. Location suggests a ringfort.

225 Cuilleen
O.S. 86:16:6 (9064 0345)
Site 026 OD 213-244
Irregular, roughly oval-shaped univallate enclosure with internal dimensions of 11m N-S by 15m E-W. Enclosing bank is earthen but with some stone in E half and averages 1m wide and 0.4m high. Possible entrance in SW where bank is lowest.

226 Cuilleen
O.S. 96:4:3 (8914 0510)
Site 041 OD 91-122
Here, a regular depressed hollow 6.2m across in diameters and 0.5m deep is enclosed by a scarp edge on all sides, except for a 2m wide gap in S.

227 Drumminaweelaun
O.S. 87:4:6 (8530 3730)
Site 020 ✔ OD 30-61
Represented only on the 1838 O.S. map, there is no trace of this roughly circular outline on the ground today. Location suggests it may have been a ringfort.

228 Fahburren
O.S. 87:16:1 (7072 1469)
Site 04203 ✔ OD 61-91
Near the centre of a large ecclesiastical enclosure (251) is situated this fairly circular stone enclosure 21m N-S by 23m E-W internally. Mostly enclosed by a stone wall spread while some facing 0.4m high gives a wall 1.5m thick. It contains the remains of a low, rectangular stone feature 8.6m E-W by 5m wide internally.

229 Glenbaun
O.S. 97:1:1 (0330 5720)
Site 050 OD 122-152
The northern half of a univallate enclosure 9m internally and 13.5m overall WNW-ESE. Its enclosing element 2m to 3m wide is stony and from 0.35m to 0.55m high; some low outer facing is visible in NE. Slight traces of an outer fosse between NE and E.

230 Glencally
O.S. 97:1:5 (0820 5120)
Site 037 OD 122-152
Roughly circular enclosure of stone and earth near the edge of a stream. Bank is best preserved along N at 1.7m wide, 0.8m high internally and 0.3m high externally, while along SW its construction is more earthen. Overall diameters of 11m N-S by 9m E-W, it reads 7.8m N-S internally. Interior contains a banked square-shaped feature about 3m across internally in the W sector.

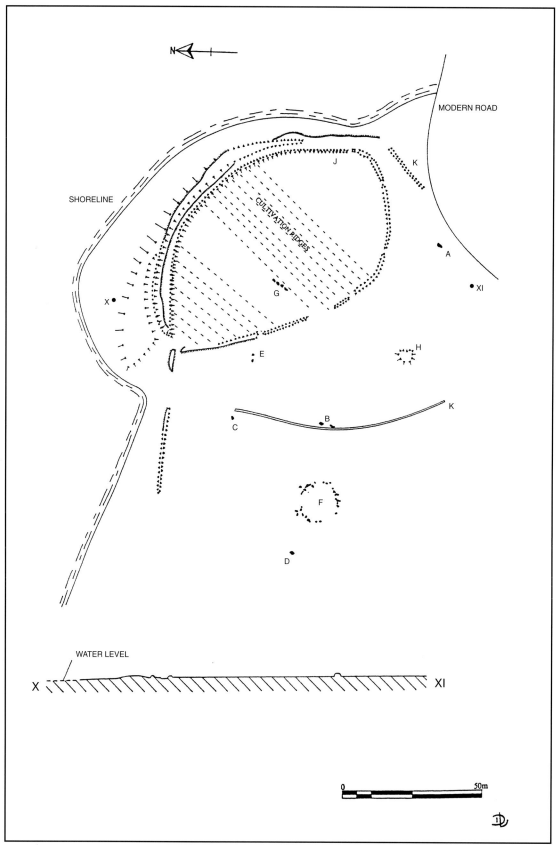

Fig 21: Coastal archaeological complex in Killadangan (37, 38, 39, 129 and 231).
A, B, C, D and E = standing stones; F = hut site; G = stone alignment;
H = Fulacht Fiadh; J = oval enclosure; K = ancient fences.

231 Killadangan
O.S. 87:11:5 (6100 2740)
Site 01401 ✔ OD 0-30
Fig. 21 + Plate 22a

Large, oval-shaped bivallate enclosure which will one day succumb to the ever increasing sea level. Enclosing banks are mostly earthen, and internal diameters measure 86m NW-SE by 54m NE-SW. Inner bank is mostly scarped but reaches 1m high internally and externally for much of NE half, while it averages 2m wide. Outer bank and fosse are only evident between NW and E. The fosse seldom exceeds 1m wide at the base, while the broad earthen outer bank averages 4m wide at the base and 0.5m high internally and externally. There are numerous **standing stones** (37) around the site; and the remains of an ancient **field system**, probably contemporary with the enclosure (64), lie outside the S to W. Later cultivation ridges occupy much of the interior.

232 Killadangan
O.S. 87:12:4 (7235 2290)
Site 03701 ✔ OD 0-30

The outline of this enclosure is no longer traceable. Visited by Frank Mitchell in 1983, he described it as a defended house site (Mitchell 1990, 125-6). A nearby shell midden (3) has also been removed.

233 Killeencoff
O.S. 87:12:6 (8910 1770)
Site 101 OD 91-122

Very poorly preserved univallate enclosure with internal diameters of 13.5m N-S by 11.5m E-W. Enclosed mainly by a moss-covered stony band 1.5m wide, it contains a small **hut** in N sector.

234 Knappaghmanagh
O.S. 88:13:2
(1390 1082) Site 05702 ✔
(1395 1110) Site 05703 ✔
OD 61-91
Plate 15b

A round **enclosure** (05702) shown on the 1838 O.S. map cannot be identified on the ground surface today. Both its location and its possession of a souterrain suggest that the original monument was a ringfort. The large **souterrain** (05703) is intact and accessible. Its main passage is aligned E-W for 7.2m, is 1.4m wide, 1.25m high at present and roofed by eight lintels. A creep on its S wall leads to a chamber 5.6m long NNE-SSW; this chamber reaches 2.1m wide and 1.6m in height and contains an air vent at S end. Near this vent another creep, followed by rough stone steps, leads to the second chamber; this measures 4.9m NNW-SSW, reaching 2.25m wide and 2m in height. Another creep leads to the last chamber which is 2.1m wide and 1.85m high; this is aligned WNW-ESE for 4.6m and is roofed by five massive lintels, unlike the previous two chambers which had four. All three chambers are permanently flooded. A tall **standing stone** at this site (50) was reputedly taken for use in the construction of Knappagh Church.

235 Knockfin
O.S. 88:9:1 (0310 2940)
Site 08601 ✔ OD 30-61

High on a sturdy ridge lies this fairly circular univallate enclosure with internal diameters of 53m NNW-SSE by 49m WSW-ENE. Perimeter is mostly overgrown yet a bank 3.4m wide, 0.55m high internally and externally can be observed along E. Some stones face the outer edge of the bank. Vegetation band of iris hints at a fosse outside bank in ENE. Interior contains a possible megalithic structure (7) to NE of centre, and some impressive banks of earth and stone. To E of centre is a D-shaped mound 0.55m high, 4.2m NW-SE by 3.1m NE-SW which is slightly hollowed. A small scarped feature 0.9m high lies against the inner face of enclosing bank in NE. Location and aspect favourable for a ringfort.

236 Letterbrock
O.S. 97:8:5 (7850 3080)
Site 027 OD 91-122

More recent activity has given this univallate enclosure an irregular outline. Its enclosing bank is mainly earthen and best defined along SW and W, at 4m wide, 1.5m high internally and 1m high externally. Only gap is 2m wide in SE. Rough overall diameters read 25m. Site interior contains the foundations of a more recent building and some associated banks.

237 Oughty
O.S. 97:15:5 (5830 0380)
Site 01301 ✔ OD 91-122

A difficult site to classify, this univallate enclosure contains a later **children's burial ground** (272), with the tallest grave marker 0.95m high said to commemorate a bishop "Crean" by some locals. The enclosing element survives as a 0.7m high scarp along NE while a more stony bank with a later wall on it forms the southern limits. An estimated N-S diameter of 40m was read. Nothing of the W half of the enclosure can be seen. Could be a ringfort and/or early monastic enclosure.

238 Streamstown
O.S. 87:8:5 (8073 3245)
Site 10502 OD 0-30

There is a very slight curving scarp from 0.4m to 0.8m high outside the N to NE and SE sector of an earthen mound (19). When complete, it would enclosure an area of roughly 30m across. Possibly the remains of a ringfort.

239 Boheh (E.D. Kilsallagh)
O.S. 96:8:2 (8130 4425)
Site 038 OD 30-61

The western portion of a sub-rectangular enclosure measures 23m N-S internally and at least 8m wide. Its narrow bank of earth and stone is only 1m wide and reaches 1m high at most. An internal bank forms a division 8m wide in NW. Just outside N a 5m wide hollow is of interest and may represent a hut.

PLACE NAMES RELATED TO POSSIBLE RINGFORTS 240-243

Place names that possibly indicate the former presence of a ringfort were collected locally. There are only four examples.

240 Carrowmore
O.S. 98:5:4 (0660 3120)
Site 038 OD 91-122
Here, the name 'lissahaun' is applied to a 14m long bank of earth and stone running ENE-WSW. Not enough surviving of the bank to determine if it forms a curve.

241 Knockaraha
O.S. 87:12:2 (8110 2480)
Site 100 OD 0-30
A local pointed to a place he said they always referred to as a fort. Partly cleared with some material also dumped here, nothing definite can be seen. This antiquity possibly gave the townland its name 'cnoc-a-rath' or the hill of the rath.

242 Lanmore
O.S. 98:1:3 (2290 5500)
Site 039 OD 91-122
The landowners always referred to this field as a 'lisheen' though no trace of any monument can be seen.

243 Liscarney
O.S. 98:5:1 (0140 4310)
Site 036 OD 91-122
Landowners stated there was something in this part of the field – they referred to it as a fort. When the field was reclaimed, they said several trailers of stone were removed.

SOUTERRAINS 244, 245

While most souterrains known in Irish archaeology are contained either within a ringfort or from early ecclesiastical enclosures, the two described below are found in isolation – though both could originally have been sited within enclosures, which are not now evident.

244 Carrowrevagh
O.S. 98:9:4 (0445 2255)
Site 032 OD 61-91
Located in a field which goes by the Irish name 'the lochromauns' (the leprechauns), it is no longer accessible. When younger, the landowner remembers entering 'a room four or five yards long with a small cubby hole at the S end. I got in through a hole in the roof'. Partly covered by a later field wall, a slight hollow in the ground can still be observed.

245 Carrowkeel
O.S. 87:6:6 (4281 2811)
Site 053 OD 0-30
Now covered in, it is formed of a passage and chamber with interconnecting creep. Passage was accessible for 3m, it was 1.22m wide at the mouth, widening to 1.5m at most internally. Oriented N-S, it was 2.15m high at most. The creep at S end was small and narrow with a trap door in its roof providing access to the chamber. In this room which runs 4.2m E-W there is a stone-built platform around the creep. Chamber contained a number of air vents and achieved 2.12m in width. (Description by Victor Buckley from *The Mayo News* 1983, p 11).

CRANNÓG 246

In general, crannógs are artificially built islands on lakes, turloughs or other inland water masses. There is only one crannóg from the survey area, and that is located on Moher Lough. While archaeological and historical evidence points to ample proof of the use of crannógs in the Early Historic and Viking times, there is also artefactual evidence linking them to the Iron Age, while Bronze Age farmers and metalworkers occasionally lived in enclosed lakeshore settlements (O'Sullivan 1998, 1). Great importance is attached to the local crannóg in the following reference, which demonstrates its strategic importance well into Medieval and later times:

> The composition describes O'Malley's country as consisting of two divisions ... and one (the eastern half) called Ilane na Moghere. It is a small island on Moher Lake on which are traces of stone buildings. It must have been a place of note to give the name to half the chiefry. We may take it to be the principal crannóg of O'Malley and place of safety for his valuables in troubled times; it may be O'Malley's island which Dermot took in 1415 (Knox 1908, 306).

246 Carrowmore
O.S. 98:5:4 (0125 3180)
Site 007 ✔ OD 61-91
Fig. 22 + Plate 19
This crannóg was constructed on a large stone pile in Moher Lake. Its edge is partly bordered by an enclosing wall, no more than three courses high externally but scattered on the inside. Heavily overgrown internally, nevertheless the foundations of a later rectangular building are clearly evident. Diameters across top measure 20m N-S by 25m E-W. The SE sector contains a stone-lined quay 8m long and 2m wide.

Plate 19: View of crannóg on Moher Lake from south (246).

Plate 20a: Reek Sunday pilgrimage at the chapel on the summit – July 2000.

Plate 20b: Leacht Mionnain, the first station on the Croagh Patrick pilgrimage – July 2000.

Plate 21a: Mr John Cummins carrying out work on toilet facilities on the summit 1992.

Plate 21b: Some members of the excavation team of 1994 at the base of Croagh Patrick.
Left to right: Michael Gibbons (Director of Survey), Owen Campbell, John Cummins,
Gerry Walsh (Director of Excavation)), Michael John Ball, William Thornton.
Missing from photograph are Frank Ryan, Brendan Walsh, Richard Gillespie, Phelim Gibbons,
Pearse de Coursey and Agnes Kerrigan.

Plate 22a: Archaeological complex between the road and the sea at Killadangan (37, 38, 83, 129 and 231).

Plate 22b: Sheeroe: This most impressive striking natural hillock in LeckŸanvey (17) from north.

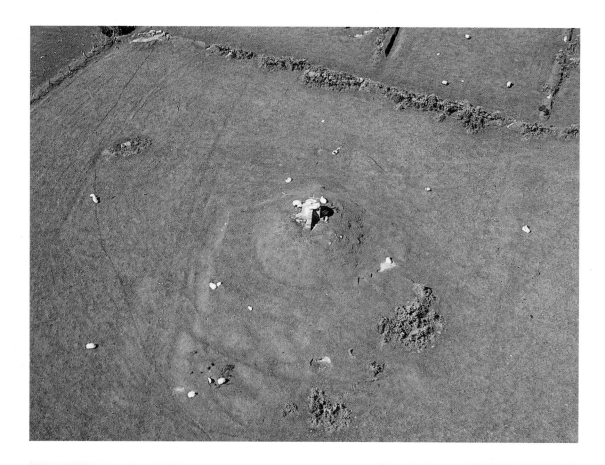

Plates 23a & 23b: Large mound at Thornhill (20) as (a) viewed from the air and (b) seen from NW. The stone feature on top contains a millstone and was created in the shape of a cross to celebrate Emancipation in 1824.

116

Plate 24a: Close-up view of the summit showing the 1905 church from N.

Plate 24b: Computer generated interpretation of Early Christian summit showing projected enclosing summit wall, external and internal features, from SW.

Plate 25a: Aerial view of bivallate ringfort in Cuilleen (208), much obscured by later walls.

Plate 25b: Aerial view of Cortoor cashel (153).

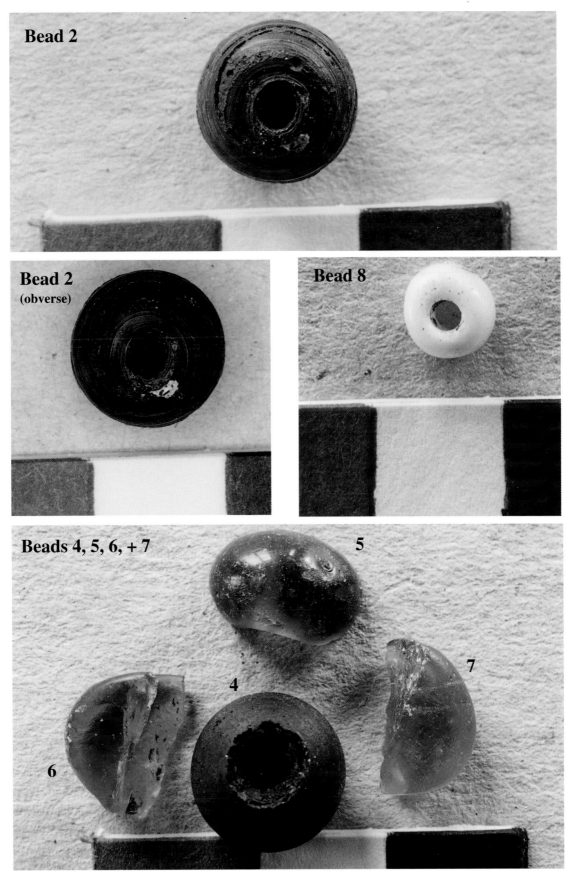

Plate 26: Some of the glass beads recovered in the 1995 excavations on the summit of Croagh Patrick; each colour on the scales represents one centimetre.

Plate 27a: Large upright pillar in Killeencoff (45).

Plate 27b: Standing stone at Liscarney (57) in a dramatic setting.

Plate 28a: Seasonal waterfall on the Glencally-Barragleanna townland boundary.

Plate 28b: Early illustration of Croagh Patrick and Westport Quay.

121

Plate 29: Aerial view of northern face of Croagh Patrick and the coastal plains with pilgrim paths from Murrisk and Leckanvey both in evidence.

Plate 30a: Stone lined mound in Murrisknaboll (18) from NE.

Plate 30b: Shell midden on the sea shore at Murrisknaboll (4).

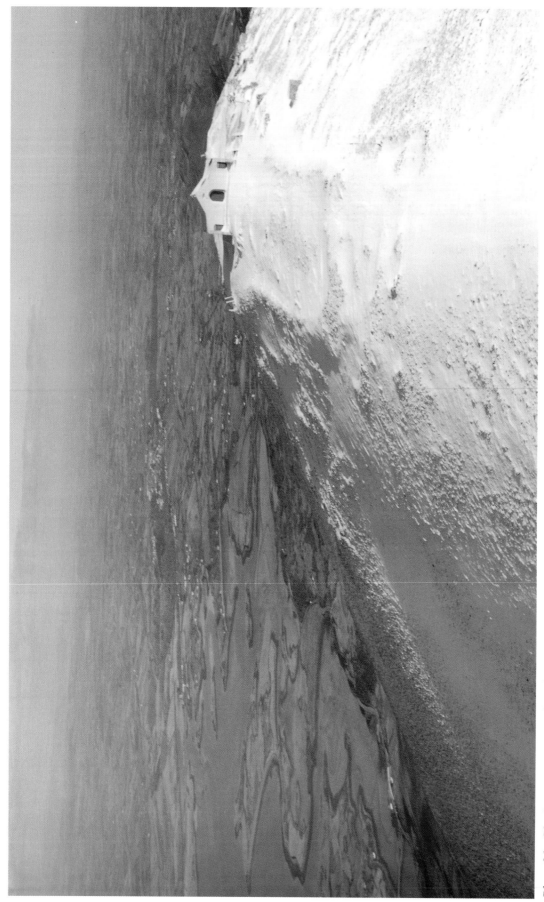

Plate 31: Glorious snow-capped peak of Croagh Patrick with the enclosing wall on the summit, and some of the hut sites clearly defined (145 + 249).

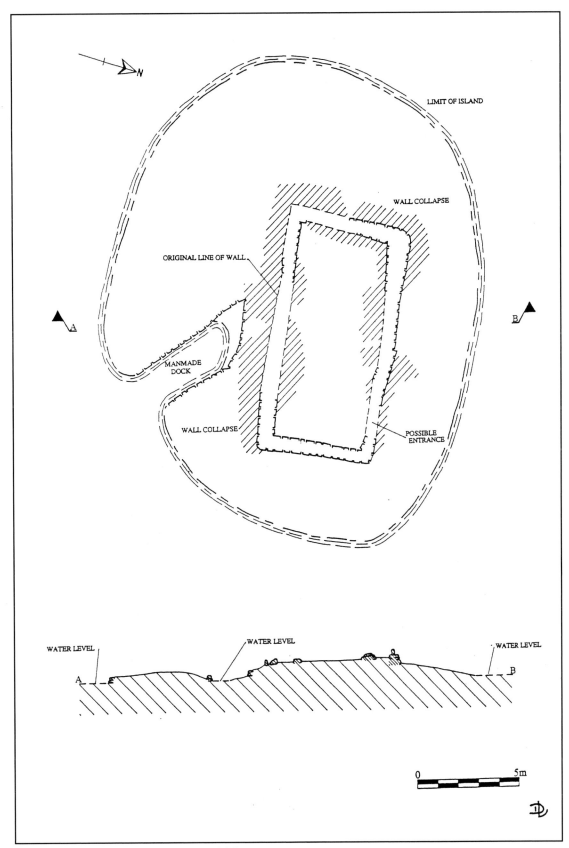

Fig. 22: Crannóg on Moher Lake (246).

EARLY ECCLESIASTICAL ENCLOSURES 247-254

These sites are looked on as highly significant monuments due to their derivation from the new religion brought to Ireland by St. Patrick; the locality has added importance also in the fact that the mountain has adopted the name of our patron saint. The occupants of some pre-Christian enclosures were converted to Christianity and these sites sometimes became actual early ecclesiastical settlements (de Paor 1978, 50). In other cases, enclosures were constructed specifically to define an early ecclesiastical establishment. For a site to be classified as an early foundation, its associated features are to include any three of the following: 1) Name of an Irish saint, 2) Enclosure, 3) Church, 4) Burial ground, 5) Holy Well, 6) Penitential Stations, 7) Leacht, or (reputed) burial place of the founder, 8) Early Christian cross slabs, 9) Bullaun stone, 10) Souterrain, 11) Upright pillar stone.

Boheh (248) is located close to the rock art outcrop (1); this, and its location practically on the ancient Togher Patrick (144), indicates the probability of major ritual or ceremonial activity hereabouts. The sites at Carrowrevagh (250) and Furgill (252) are located in similar settings, built into the side of a ridge. However, the damp, poor quality land around the latter, makes it today rather inaccessible. Only Glaspatrick, Croagh Patrick and Oughavale have continued as consecrated grounds, though mass was recently celebrated at Furgill for the first time in living memory. Burials still occur at Oughavale and Glaspatrick, while most of the sites, since the time of their deconsecration, have been used for the burial of unbaptised children.

Outside of the survey area, early monastic sites at Kilgeever (O.S. 86, 006) and Caher Island (O.S. 94, 003) have been traditionally associated with the pilgrimage to Croagh Patrick (O'Donovan 1838, 159). Two further sites at Lankill (O.S. 98, 003) and Carrowkennedy (O.S. 97, 014) possess extensive remains and are located just outside the survey area to the east. One of the largest (30 acres) and most important Early Christian sites in County Mayo is that at Mayo Abbey. Originally founded by St. Colman of Lindisfarne, it acquired the greatest reputation of all the monasteries in this county down to the twelfth century (Knox 1908, 35). The same author, in a general reference to the seventh century, mentions that the Columban monks were settled at Oughavale (1908, 35), thence the origins of St. Columcille's well; while elsewhere he refers to the old church at Cloonpatrick representing the Patrician foundation (ibid., 305). These references and names associated with Oughavale–Ardoley–Churchfield suggest that the older original foundation was on the lower ground to the N, with the new settlement centred around the current surviving church to S.

These sites had all probably been abandoned by the tenth century as there are no known records of any of their ecclesiastical establishments being plundered by Viking raids, and the nearest find from Viking times is a hoard of silver arm rings and ingots, and one gold ingot, discovered on the shores of Newport Bay in the townland of Cushalogurt (Sheehan 1995; 168, 200).

247 Ardoley – Churchfield
O.S. 87:12:3
(8780 2800) Site 023 ✔
(8826 2854) Site 024 ✔
(8780 2721) Site 039 ✔
(8855 2780) Site 040 ✔
OD 0-30

Commonly referred to as **Oughavale graveyard**, one large ecclesiastical complex here is probably composed of two former Early Christian settlements. While the enclosures are no longer evident, they seem to have centred themselves on either side of the main road through here. Both St. Patrick and St. Columcille are associated with these sites.

To the N of the road, very little survives; a small **church** which stood in Ardoley is no longer evident, while the only upstanding structure is a large, stone-built, communal, gabled grave. A large **bullaun** near this is called 'Gloonpatrick' and its waters are reputedly a cure for warts.

Across the road to the S the **church** remains are those of a medieval structure; its W gable together with parts of the N (4.9m) and S (10.8m) walls are all that survive. Construction is of undressed and roughly dressed stonework, laid down in an uncoursed or roughly coursed fashion. Apart from a plain doorway and splayed window on S wall, there are few features of note.

An extension to the W gable end appears to have been used most recently for burials and contains a partly dressed twelfth to thirteenth century doorway.

The **holy well** near here is named 'St. Columcille's Well' on the 1838 and later O.S. maps. It lies at the base of an enormous elm tree and is enclosed by a drystone wall; this wall contains a small alcove on its inner face, near the entrance at W. O'Donovan mentioned a flag at the well that had been used as a cursing stone, but had been broken before his visit in 1838 (O'Donovan Letters, 215).

A second ecclesiastical presence at the site is indicated by the name Oughavale, which has been broken down to 'Nua Chongbhal' and translated as new settlement or habitation.

248 Boheh (E.D. Knappagh)
O.S. 97:4:6 (9150 5100)
Site 019 ✔ OD 61-91

Located 80m to the S of the rock art stone of Boheh (1) and on the edge of the Togher Patrick (144), these ecclesiastical remains contain a **church foundations, burial ground, holy well** and five **cross-inscribed slabs**.

The **church** is located in NW sector of a graveyard, but no clear construction is evident as the remains are scant. Aligned NNE-SSW, it yields internal dimensions of 4.2 by 2.2m. Two erect **cross slabs** stand on the inner face of ESE wall, with a further two on WNW wall, facing each other. There is a fifth slab 100m to the W on lower ground, which is much taller than the others (0.65m high); this slab accompanies a stone grave 2.3m NW-SE by 1.7m wide and 0.5m high. All the incised crosses are narrow, shallow and simple.

Burial ground measures 30m NE-SW by 24m wide, and graves are represented by upright markers, stone-lined graves or a combination of both. All markers are simple and average 0.2m high.

It is uncertain if the scarp 2.4m high along SW represents part of the ecclesiastical enclosure. A later wall here contains a stone-lined hollow, which some locals referred to as a **holy well**.

It is said children were buried at this site up until the 1950s.

The rock art and a standing stone to S (27) show there was already pre-Christian activity at this location.

249 Croagh Patrick Summit
O.S. 87:14:4 (2560 0430)
Site 044 ✔ OD 762-793
Fig. 2 + Plate 2 + Plate 31
There is sufficient evidence to show that the summit of Croagh Patrick was functioning for some period as an early monastic settlement. The enclosing wall of the earlier rampart would have been more than sufficient to enclose this new monastic settlement. Aligned E-W, an Early Christian oratory was described earlier (see excavation report pages 18-22), and this lies 10m from the rampart wall spread at N and 27m from E. Temple Patrick represented on earlier maps was probably another religious building and it stood close to this oratory, while the mountain top rubble possibly covers over the remains of further church buildings.

The **Leaba Patrick** or St. Patrick's Bed was his traditional resting place and consists of a slight, apparently natural, hollow area which could represent the remains of a further collapsed structure. The highest ground at the site just E of this is occupied by a trigonometrical station, though the earlier church and later oratory are on relatively high ground. Nothing else survives at ground level from Early Christian times. The area enclosed by the collapsed mountain top wall measures 154m E-W; it reaches 30m wide near the eastern end and narrows considerably to 18m at the western end.

One wonders how long the site survived as a practising settled ecclesiastical centre, and what caused its eventual demise. Was it frequent inclement weather and inhospitable surroundings, or the fact that practising Christians continuously came on pilgrimage and to visit, making this secluded retreat more of an open house?

250 Carrowrevagh
O.S. 97:12:5 (8180 1850)
Site 012 ✔ OD 91-122
Similar to the site at Furgill (252) in the method of building into the side of a ridge, its northern part was damaged many years ago through reclamation. Enclosing bank of earth and stone averages 2m to 3m wide and from 0.5m to 1.2m high and is only evident from NE to W. An internal E-W diameter of 55m was read.

Burial ground within its E interior measures 19m N-S and E-W and is enclosed by a stony bank. Original **church** was probably in this area but not a trace can be seen today. It does contain a well-built **altar** (leacht), 0.75m high and 2m across. A number of well-rounded cursing stones lie on this altar while a damaged **cross-inscribed slab** lies against its base. Graves or grave markers are not clearly identifiable. (Round stones like those here come from the sea shore along many of the strands on the S side of Clew Bay).

251 Fahburren
O.S. 87:16:1 (7070 1470)
Site 04201 ✔ OD 61-91
Fig. 23

In a wonderfully scenic, undulating, partly wooded area stands this large **enclosure** with internal diameters of 87m NNE-SSW by 110m E-W (roughly). Enclosing earthen bank is stone faced at intervals while there is a flat, earthen stone-faced ledge outside the enclosing bank from NW to NE sector. Interior contains a circular stone **enclosure** (228) near the centre, and low foundations of a **church** 6.4m E-W by 3.9m N-S internally are located within a slightly elevated ancient burial area. Graves in this area are represented by stone-lined graves or simple grave markers 0.45m high at most. Just W of the church foundations is a **bullaun stone** 0.75m long, 0.57m wide and 0.22m thick, whose hollow is 0.35m across and 0.18m deep. There is a stone **cairn** 0.5m high at most and of uncertain antiquity outside E side of church. Church and burial ground are enclosed by a later graveyard wall, built to receive burials of the Buchanan family of Prospect House, which is located a short distance to NW. Parts of SE and SW interior are low-lying and marshy, while part of an ancient internal bank runs roughly E-W through the site. There is clear evidence for an entrance against the later graveyard wall near NE. The townland and the area are better known locally as Prospect.

252 Furgill
O.S. 96:4:4 (7270 4550)
Site 013 ✔ OD 30-61
Plate 12b

This oval-shaped **enclosure** is set against and into the N slopes of a pronounced ridge and skirted by poor boggy ground to the N and E. Enclosing wall in northern half is collapsed and in places difficult to identify; its southern half is scooped out of the hillside, and the ensuing scarp is faced with a dry stone wall 1.5m high on average. Rough internal diameters measure 24m N-S by 32m E-W. Site interior is naturally divided into three various levels, highest at S end and lowest at NE. The central and NE sectors contain **burials** – these are represented by graves or markers, and none exceed 0.4m high. A nearly circular **cairn** 2.8m across and 0.8m high in the ENE interior formed a leacht or altar while some whitethorns grow along its edge.

The remains of **St. Patrick's Well** can be seen 30m to NNW. It appears to have dried up and is enclosed now by a later stone wall. A fine **bullaun stone** (258) is located in W sector embedded into the ground.

253 Glaspatrick
O.S. 87:10:1 (2810 2540)
Site 028 ✔ OD 0-30
Plate 32

Features at this site include **church remains, burial ground** and **holy well** while oral tradition and some documentary sources refer to St. Patrick's charioteer being buried here. Church survives in poor condition with very large stones used in the wall construction along N. Mortar from this wall shows that gravel and shell were used. While E and W walls are in poor condition, S wall is considerably better, reaching 1.9m high internally. While burials, grave slabs and markers are evidenced within and outside the church, none gave a date earlier than 1889.

Toberglas, the **holy well**, is bordered by a later drystone wall, with a small alcove or niche near its entrance in W.

We were told locally of a tall engraved pillar stone that stood within the graveyard, which went missing many years ago.

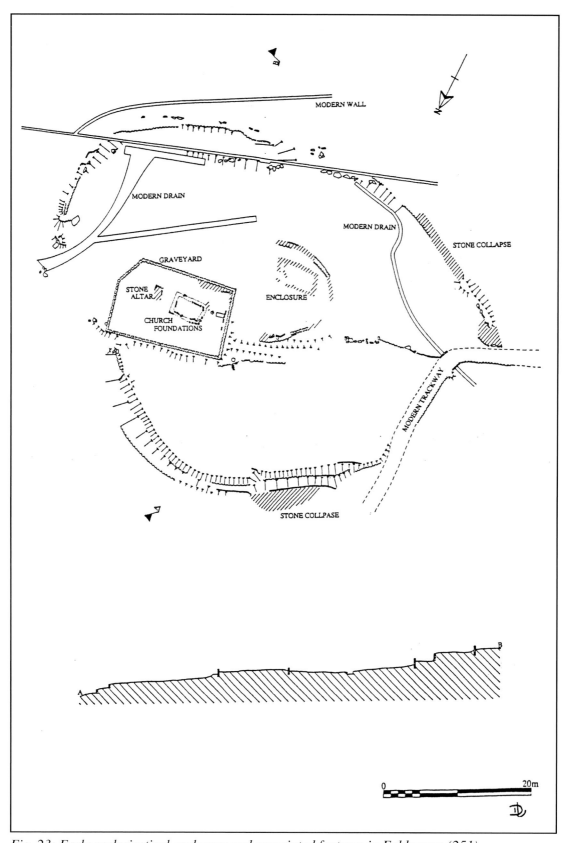

Fig. 23: Early ecclesiastical enclosure and associated features in Fahburren (251). (Known locally as Prospect).

254 Knappaghmanagh
O.S. 88:13:2 (1500 0936)
Site 058 ✔ OD 30-61
Plate 13a

The monastic **enclosure** here is oval-shaped, 72m N-S by 57m E-W internally. Enclosing bank of earth and stone is best preserved from SE to SSW, reaching 5m wide and 1.7m high internally and externally; a shallow fosse 2m wide can be seen outside this sector. A circular **enclosure** (in S) 11.5m N-S by 16.5m E-W internally was used as a **children's burial ground**; its bank is earthen, level internally and reaches 0.7m high externally. Rough graves and markers cover much of the area, with the latter never exceeding 0.35m high. The site contains part of a well executed cross slab depicting a figure with upraised arms, the best known Early Christian cross slab from the survey area. Burial ground contains a D-shaped annex against its N sector. An **altar** or leacht in the S sector of the main enclosure reaches 3.2m NW-SE, 1.7m wide and 0.6m high.

Lying 13m to SSW is a small **enclosure** of equal, or possibly greater, antiquity 11m N-S by 13m E-W overall. It is enclosed by a bank of earth and stone, similar in construction to the main enclosure; this bank averages 2.5m to 3.5m wide, 0.8m high internally and 1.2m high externally. It has a gap 2.6m wide in E, while internal diameters measure 6m N-S by 7m E-W.

Plate 32: Aerial view of ecclesiastical centre at Glaspatrick (253).

BULLAUN STONES 255-261

Bullaun stones are stones with one or more hollows or basins excavated in them. They are a prominent feature of many monastic sites and are present in three of the above ecclesiastical sites. However, a small number of other hollow stones were pointed out locally, whose basins usually bear the name of St. Patrick. Bullaun stones were used in an ecclesiastical context as holy water receptacles or fonts, yet some would have been used earlier as a primitive corn grinding apparatus. The bullauns at Ardoley (256), Fahburren (251) and Furgill (258) are located within definite Early Christian contexts.

255 Bellataleen
O.S. 87:10:6 (4265 2164)
Site 113 OD 30-61
This irregular hollow 0.26 by 0.12m and 0.05m deep, in outcropping rock, has been referred to as St. Patrick's footprint.

256 Ardoley
O.S. 87:12:3 (8765 2800)
Site 02303 OD 0-30
This bullaun is located on the N side of the Louisburgh-Westport road, within the monastic site at Ardoley or Oughavale (247). It is large and heavy, of red sandstone, and set in a boulder at least 1.2m long, 1.15m wide and 0.16m thick. One half of the hollow is partly broken yet a distinct basin 0.65m wide and 0.13m deep is visible.

257 Cuilleen
O.S. 96:4:3 (8334 5810)
Site 039 OD 61-91
A hollow 0.15m by 0.1m and 0.05m deep is found in an irregular boulder on E side of a gravel road. Locals stated that the hollow, which appears natural, was the imprint of St. Patrick's knee, as he moved west from the mountain.

258 Furgill
O.S. 96:4:4 (7260 4550)
Site 01306 OD 30-60
In the W sector of the Early Christian enclosure (252). A very regular hollow 0.32m across and 0.1m deep is set into a large irregular block c. 1.1m long, 0.58m wide and 0.24m thick, which is partly buried in the ground.

259 Mullagh
O.S. 96:4:1 (6955 5361)
Site 037 OD 30-61
Another hollow, partly artificial, partly cut associated with St. Patrick's knee. In a large boulder on E side of a damp disused boreen, it is oval-shaped, 0.17m by 0.13m across the top and 0.05m deep. Locals recall people blessing themselves with its waters.

260 Oughty
O.S. 97:15:1 (5305 1087)
Site 033 OD 91-122
Plate 33
Moved from the bank of a nearby ringfort (218) to S, this almost symmetrical hollow reads 0.33m by 0.3m across the top and 0.13m deep. Set in a large heavy boulder 1.15m long by 0.9m wide by 0.7m thick.

261 Oughty
O.S. 97:11:5 (5820 1576)
Site 061 OD 91-122
A natural hollow in rock outcrop on E side of a mountain stream is locally known as St. Patrick's Knee, though it is under water for much of the year. An oval depression 0.31m by 0.26m and 0.19m deep can be seen here. Locals heard of people in former times blessing themselves with water from this basin.

There is also the bullaun stone in the ecclesiastical enclosure at **Fahburren (251)** already dealt with under those site types.

Plate 33: Present location of large bullaun stone in Oughty (260).

MEDIEVAL STONE BUILDINGS 262, 263

There are two buildings in the survey area which date from the Medieval period.

1. FRIARY

From the time of the arrival of Christianity in Ireland to the beginning of the twelfth century, very few changes had occurred in Irish religious life. The early Celtic monasteries just discussed were laid out in a rather random casual plan, and perhaps this began to reflect itself in people's attitudes and adherence to their religion. For different reasons, the 12th century church in Ireland was undergoing change, and this change is best reflected in the arrival of the established orders to these shores. It was St. Malachy of Armagh who through his disciples helped set up a Cistercian Abbey at Mellifont, Co. Louth, in 1142, the first of these orders to arrive in Ireland. Like a Roman villa, these new religious houses were laid out in an ordered fashion with the main buildings, including the church, arranged around an ambulatory or cloister arcade. These orders were also characterised by their adherence to rules and regulations, while all had their own dress code.

In the sequence of church construction, Murrisk was rather late, not having been founded until 1457. It was established following a letter from Pope Callistus III granting permission to Hugh O'Malley, an Augustinian friar of the house of Corpus Christi at Banada in Co. Sligo, to establish a church and friary at Murrisk. Thady O'Malley, who was the chief of the area, reputedly granted lands at Murrisk for this church foundation. It is uncertain how long the Murrisk religious community survived in the area; however, all available references appear to suggest the early nineteenth century. A report of 1801 by the Archbishop of Tuam stated that there was one Augustinian at Murrisk (probably appointed by the Provincial to hold possession in the hope of better times for the friary). Some chalices connected with Murrisk Friary or its brethren have previously been mentioned in the section on Historical References, with two of these dated 1635 and 1724 respectively.

Plate 34: Drawing of Murrisk Friary from Grose's Antiquities of Ireland *(1791).*
Courtesy of The National Library of Ireland.

262 Murrisk Friary
O.S. 87:10:3 (3850 2771)
Site 031 ✔ OD 0-30
𝔐𝔲𝔯𝔯𝔦𝔰𝔨 𝔄𝔟𝔟𝔢𝔶 (in ruins)
Plate 34

The church is aligned E-W for 18.2m (including tower at W end) and 6.1m wide internally with the remains of domestic buildings to N. Construction is of dressed regular masonry, generally evenly coursed. At the western end the tall tower is unusual in that it has been built within the church itself, supported on the west wall and with its corresponding parallel wall to the E today forming the W wall of the church interior. The surviving doorway on this wall is inserted into a partly blocked up embrasure 2.88m wide and of a considerable height. Features from the church include:

E wall – With ornate window divided by four transoms. Altar of stone beneath it is intact.

S wall – One narrow pointed arched doorway in a splayed embrasure near the western end.
– One ogee headed, one twin-ogee headed and a two-light rectangular window, all set in splayed embrasures.
– Coping stones high up externally. All the stonework above this, including crennelation, is of a later date.
– Serene carved stone head on outer face of wall, facing towards Croagh Patrick.
– A piscina and a damaged sedillia towards E end.
– Putlog holes internally and externally.

W wall – Incorporated a later tower, with part of a narrow window high up on its S wall.

N wall – One ogee headed window; putlog holes internally and externally, some corbells externally, string course high up on western half (also found on domestic buildings to N of church) and a plain narrow doorway leading to the sacristy at E end.

Adjacent to the sacristy is the Chapter Room, while a room of similar size with its doorway in the N wall is immediately to the N of this. Architectural features from this northern series of buildings include flat headed, round, pointed and ogee headed windows, fireplaces, external corbels, slop stones and various doors including one in the porch between the church and the sacristy which contains a hanging eye. A passage between the church and sacristy has stairs which lead to dormitories on the first floor.

The church architecture shows it to have been built about the middle of the fifteenth century. The wing extending northwards from the church is later in construction, with the inserted tower at the W end later still and probably contemporary with the crennelations on the S wall.

2. CASTLE

Castle construction was introduced into Ireland following the Anglo-Norman invasion of 1169. The first castles built were of timber, and the earthworks which held them could take the form of either a motte, motte and bailey or a ringwork (Sweetman 1999, 3-32). We have one recognised motte and bailey from Mayo in the townland of Castlereagh near Irishtown (S.M.R. 112:036), while a recently detected earthwork from Cloonbaul townland (S.M.R. 99: 100) in Mayo Abbey parish resembles a ringwork castle (Mayo Abbey Survey 1996). While stone castles were built in Anglo-Norman parts of the country from the beginning of the conquest, the Anglo-Normans had little impact on Mayo. The local castle of Belclare was located in the heartland of the O'Malley Lordship. By the fifteenth century, when the Anglo-Normans were deeply Gaelicized, the building of stone castles was almost universal, even in Gaelic areas. The large stone castles were mostly built by this time, and the most common form was the Tower House. These were self-contained towers of three to six stories.

263 Belclare Castle
O.S. 87:12:1 (7462 2625)
Site 038 ✔ OD 0-30
Castle (site of)

No trace of this castle can be seen today. Located on a high elbow of land on the eastern side of the Owenwee estuary, it was not represented on the 1838 O.S. map. A later Bleach Mill and Cotton Factory here probably used most of its stone work in their construction. References to the castle at Belclare are scarce, though one from Knox (1908, 305) states that O'Malleys town could be taken to have been about Belclare – perhaps based around the castle there. Within this territory, the O'Malleys alone possessed castle, with that at Belclare going with the chieftainship. Other castles in the possession of this family around the sixteenth century included one at Caher-na-Mart (near where Westport House now stands), one in Carramore townland just west of Louisburgh town and one near the pier on Clare Island.

One member of the O'Malley family, Granuaile or Grace, is remembered as a strong-willed individual from sixteenth century Mayo. She was of the Gaelic O'Malley clan whose associations with the sea can be traced back to Celtic times (Chambers 1983, 26). Among their maritime activities were fishing, piracy and plunder, mercenary work in various wars and disputes, trading journeys and the provision of a pilot service to foreign vessels. Granuaile's unique ability is evidenced in the fact that she had been accepted as captain of the fleet, not only by her two husbands but by all the various clans in the locality, over which she held undisputed sway (ibid., 26-27). One of her sons, Theobald Bourke (or Toby of the Ships), showed a remarkable instinct for survival during the turbulent sixteenth to seventeenth century and achieved the distinguished honour of becoming First Viscount Mayo early in the seventeenth century.

CHILDREN'S BURIAL GROUNDS 264-272

The practice of burying infants and young children at specific unconsecrated sites has been carried out in Ireland over the past few centuries or so. Local people can recall the interment of infants up to the early 1960s in places, with the actual burial often carried out at nightfall. Regrettably, still-born infants and those who died before baptism were deemed unsuitable and unworthy of a Christian burial. In some instances, bigger children who perhaps had yet to receive the sacrament of communion, were also interred at such sites when they died. Graves are usually represented by box-like stone piles or simple upright stones as markers, or often a combination of both. Abandoned Early Christian foundations which had become deconsecrated were a favoured location for children's burial grounds and examples locally are found at Boheh (248), Fahburren (251), Furgill (252) and Knappaghmanagh (254). Ringforts have also been utilised for this practice of burial, perhaps reflecting the superstitious belief of many of our ancestors that when children died at a young age it was the 'faeries' who had taken them – and by burying them at the 'fairy fort' they were perhaps simply giving credence to this belief. These unconsecrated or deconsecrated burial areas are known as cillíní or ceallúnaigh in different parts of the county. In recent years, many such sites have been reconsecrated.

264 Boheh (E.D. Knappagh)
O.S. 97:4:6 (9140 5200)
Site 019 ✔ OD 61-91
A heavy concentration of upright stones, averaging 0.2m high, indicate the burials at the monastic settlement here (248). Graves occur within most of the former ecclesiastical area, with a notable concentration around the church remains in NW. The site is heavily overgrown.

265 Brackloon
O.S. 87:16:3 (8562 1463)
Site 08802 OD 61-91
No trace of any burial in the cashel (149) which some locals state was used for burying children. However, the cashel interior is extremely overgrown and neglected.

266 Fahburren
O.S. 87:16:1 (7080 1480)
Site 04204 ✔ OD 61-91
Lisheen (Children's Burial Ground)
Contained within the monastic enclosure (251) and today also enclosed by the Buchanan family graveyard wall. Unclear if all the simple markers, which reach 0.45m high, are those of infant burials. Graves and markers are very concentrated and cover an area 16m N-S by 19m E-W. They are mainly found to N and E of the church foundations.

267 Killaghoor
O.S. 88:6:1 (2965 3792)
Site 034 ✔ OD 30-61
Contained within a very roughly defined circular enclosure 28m across, graves and markers are confined to the central and southern parts. Grave markers reach 0.36m high and are aligned N-S.

268 Killadangan
O.S. 87:11:3 (6440 2295)
Site 034 ✔ OD 30-61
Lisheenaneeve (Children's Burial Ground)
Named Lisheenaneeve children's burial ground (1920) or graveyard (1901), this wall-enclosed sub-circular site measures roughly 16m across. Burials are represented by simple, upright markers (0.4m high) or stone-lined graves. A cairn 2.5m in diameter and 0.8m high stands out in SW sector. This is a much overgrown site.

269 Knappaghmanagh
O.S. 88:13:2 (0149 0910)
Site 0580 ✔ OD 30-61
Simple, upright markers or stone-lined graves represent the burials and a rough count calculated thirty or so. It is bordered by a sub-circular banked enclosure 11m across internally, which is low internally. Markers average 0.2 to 0.35m high. Portion of a most ornate Early Christian slab shows a weird human figure, whose body is formed by a ringed cross, taking the appearance of a shield. Its arms are raised, with the hands placed on the head. Other cross motifs and cup marks decorate the slab.

270 Kilsallagh Lower
O.S. 86:12:5 (8150 1995)
Site 00902 OD 0-30
Local tradition maintains that young children were buried within the cashel here (173) but there are no surface indications of irregularities on the ground surface or of any stone markers.

271 Letterbrock
O.S. 97:8:5 (7984 3443)
Site 031 OD 91-122
Landowner stated there was a children's burial ground in this location, though no trace can be seen today. The tradition of burials here had passed to the speaker through two generations.

272 Oughty
O.S. 97:15:5 (5945 0370)
Site 01302 ✔ OD 61-91
Contained in the E sector of a univallate enclosure (237), a banked wall encloses the site. Its outline is roughly circular measuring 13m N-S by 16.5m E-W internally. Upright markers average 0.4m high, but one standing 0.95m high near the centre is connected to a bishop "Crean", according to some local tradition. Markers are aligned E-W in eastern half and NW-SE in western half. Also contains a stony rectangular outline 2.5m N-S by 1.8m E-W in W sector.

MISCELLANEOUS

CHARCOAL PITS and IRON WORKING

273 Brackloon
O.S. 87:16:6
Site 123

274 Knappagh More
O.S. 88:13:1 (0110 0600)
Site 053 ✔ OD 60-91

At three different locations in the heart of Brackloon Wood, remains of charcoal pits have been exposed. Over the years, storm force winds have resulted in the uprooting of some trees and this damage has led to these charcoal areas being uncovered. Charcoal samples taken for radio-carbon dating have produced dates in the sixteenth and seventeenth century. It appears likely that the old iron mill or foundry at Knappaghmore was in full swing during these years and that charcoal would have been the fuel used, as timber or peat would be unable to produce the same degree of heat needed for iron smelting. An 1802 Statistical Survey of the area mentions vast quantities of iron ore in the barony of Murrisk (McParlan 1802, 20). It is known that Colonel John Browne of Westport, who was appointed Lord Lieutenant in Mayo in 1689, was supplying cannon balls, iron and tools of his own manufacture to the garrisons of Athlone and Galway; at the same time he had orders to requisition men and provisions for the army and for the garrisons at Galway and Inishbofin (Mulloy 1981, 34). One reference mentions that the tools, arms and cannon balls supplied by Col. Browne to the garrison of Sligo consisted of 220 shovels, 56 spades, 85 pickaxes and 965 cannon balls of three to five pounds in weight (The Marquess of Sligo 1981, 97). A memorandum accompanying this list includes other weapons including sword blades unground, swords, muskets, firelocks without barrels and braced speararms (ibid.). The foundry at Knappaghmore, being on John Browne's estate, must have been the focal point for the manufacture of the tools referred to above, and the immediate surroundings have heavy concentrations of iron slag, along with stone and other material which appear to have been vitrified. Two extant stone kilns were associated with this extensive iron-working site where recent testing (Excavations Bulletin 2001) revealed a build-up of waste material at least 1.8 meters deep. Apart from Knappaghmore, the nearest known foundry is one three kilometres NW of Newport town in the aptly named townland of Furnace.

DEERPARK

Deerparks are large walled enclosed areas so constructed for the keeping of herds of deer. They were a common Medieval feature from the thirteenth century English landscape and were introduced to Ireland by the Normans along with fallow deer and rabbits (Mac Gabhaun 1990, 4). Practically every county in Ireland contains at least one deerpark. Early references to deerparks are scant, yet informative. The earliest account, dated 1305, comes from the calendar of justiciary rolls and concerned a legal case between Richard de Burgo (The Earl of Ulster) and one William Waspayl (Mills (ed.) 1914, 133). William was charged with the poaching of deer, of breaking down the fencing which enclosed the compound and of digging a pit outside the deerpark itself. In addition, he was charged with threatening the parker and of stealing a spear from the hands of the parker's son.

There are two 'Deerpark' townlands in the Westport area, with one in the Murrisk area of most concern here. Named Deerpark West, it is a rectangularly-shaped townland and was enclosed by a well-built impressive wall, with the main entrance pillars and gate still surviving at the western end of N wall. The wall of the Deerpark served also as the townland boundary wall in most sectors – some of the wall has been removed along the southern end of the townland, while most of the remainder is still standing. Two square-shaped pens or deer folds *(see Plate 14b)*, built of stone, can still be seen near the southern end of the townland, while an outline resembling a third is evident in the north central part of the townland on the 1901 O.S. map. The townland is one of poor undulating damp ground occupied by two small lakes; it is likely that the deerpark is an associated feature of Westport House estate, the first house being built in 1650, possibly on the foundations of an earlier castle.

MILLS

Water mills were found scattered throughout the area with well known examples at **Cloonagh** where several ruined buildings and the mill race are extant. Variously there were woollen, bleach, flour and corn mills here at different times and part of their structures are still standing, with one of the original millstones incorporated into a later wall turret around the Cloonagh Health Farm.

There was also a bleach and corn mill at Belclare, close to the site of the former castle (263), but not a trace of either can be seen today. On the western side of the mountain, there is a millstone quarry in the townland of Boheh which contains numerous incomplete mill stones, while the site of the original mill where the Bellakip river crosses the Cartoor road was pointed out by a local. A millstone, possibly from the long removed Leckanvey mill, has been built into the prominently sited Emancipation Cross in Thornhill (20). The mill which stood in Ardmore was up to six or seven stories high and was later used as a cement store until 1929 (pers.com. J. Mulloy). Seventeen millstones from the site have been dispersed locally, with four now located in the Clew Bay Heritage Centre at the Quay and many of the remainder distributed among members of the Mulloy family, Westport. Other mills once stood at Brackloon, Bellataleen, Carrownalurgan, Knappaghmore, Ardmore and Liscarney, with a millstone from the latter on a wall across the road from the Post Office there. Part of an unfinished mill stone lies on the S side of the road to Lug Village in Cuilleen townland.

LIME KILNS AND OTHER REMAINS

Until the middle of the last century, lime was burned by most farmers and used for applying to the land and for whitewashing, and nearly every farm had its own lime kiln. Today many are still surviving, though neglected; one in Cuilleen near the village of Lug necessitated transporting limestone at least three miles to supply the kiln (local landowner). While those on individual farms were self-sufficient lime kilns, that in Fahburren on the approach to Prospect House was obviously used for mass production, supplying lime for the entire estate and possibly beyond. It reaches 4m high at the front where it is 6m across. A road serviced its upper section so that fuel for burning and the limestone itself could be transported more easily.

From the recent past there are a number of **quays** along the coast at Carrowkeeran, Drumminaweelaun, Leckanvey, Murrisk Demesne and Murrisknaboll, while the **Railway Viaduct Bridge** on the grounds of Rice College, Westport is a superb remnant of public works from the nineteenth century. Small prominent coastal **turrets** of recent date sit on drumlins in Drumminaweelaun and Streamstown. The remains of a stone building in Lanmore was shown as **Tower** (in ruins) on the 1920 O.S. map. It was built on naturally rocky foundations and occupies the driest part of the field. Part of an obscure curving wall with outer stone facing 0.4m high can be made out. When complete, this would give an overall diameter of 5m. It comprises mainly grassed-over rubble and earth and is highest along S at 2.6m above field level.

Chapter 5

The Landscape of the Monuments

The study area is and has been one dominated both physically and spiritually by Croagh Patrick and to a lesser extent by its foothills. Due to the mountain's perfectly triangular profile and its prominence and domination of the skyline in the region, Croagh Patrick would have formed a natural landmark long before the arrival here of man. Extensive and panoramic views from the summit would have further enhanced the importance of the mountain when eventually man first settled in the area.

Natural resources from the survey area which could have been utilised include gold, serpentine and soapstone, while its location on the edge of Clew Bay would have allowed easy access to fish as a food source. Hazel has occurred in heavy concentrations in the pollen analysis from earliest times and its nuts would have provided a valuable food supplement. Landscapes which won't have altered significantly since earliest times include the mountain block of Croagh Patrick, the numerous drumlins to its east and the maritime zone between the mountainous wedge and Clew Bay. Greater variations in the natural landscape must have occurred in the vast tracts of peat to the south of the mountain and in areas which have experienced intermittent periods as natural woodlands – changes which were doubtless caused by the presence or absence of man.

Beneath the mountain, its foothills form a rough E-W alignment and vary between 120m and 360m in height. In common with the mountain, they are generally heather-clad and rocky, and beneath the foothills, an abundance of drumlins supports better quality soil. These foothills and drumlins presented themselves as ideal locations for settlement. Rivers and their tributaries are plentiful, with the mountain block forming a huge natural reservoir for rain and sub-surface water.

Early prehistoric activity is suggested at the mountain in one certain monument type: impressive cairns stand on its shoulders to the ESE (23) and SW (21) of the summit; the former, measuring 10.5m by 7m and from 2m to 3m high, stands alone while the latter is a group of three cairns, the largest of which is 11m across and 3.2m high. Neither site displays cairn revetment though later pilgrim activity may have altered their original appearance. Both are located at the base of the cone of the mountain in areas of rather restricted aspect, and both are adjacent to ancient routes leading to and from the mountain top (144). The location of the three cairns (21) where four townland boundaries meet must also be of significance, and strategically they can be compared with those on sacred mountains (The Paps) in Kerry, though the latter actually crown the peaks (Condit [ed.] 2000). Two groups of cairns in Slievenaglasha, The Burren, Co. Clare, are situated along the extreme edge of a high rocky plateau. These are closely related morphologically to the Croagh Patrick examples; however, the relatively good aspect of the former group contrasts with the rather restricted views from the latter. Mention must also be made here of the extremely large and prominently located cairn at Sheean (22), one mile to the east of Westport. This commands extensive views of vast areas to the N and E and, to the W, over the approaches to Croagh Patrick.

Two enclosures from the mountain are also closely related geographically with the two cairn groups. One (220) forms an irregular enclosure 75m N-S by 82m E-W around the three cairns at Roilig Mhuire (21). While later pilgrims traced its outline as part of the mountain pilgrimage, it may originally have formed a ritual ceremonial enclosure connected to the cairns. Likewise, it is possible that the mountain summit has been enclosed from prehistoric times, and that chief among the reasons for creating the cairns beneath the cone was the presence of an early ritual enclosure on the summit.

141

Similarities between these local cairns and that at Poulawack, Co. Clare are not evident superficially. Excavations at the latter uncovered a cist burial dated 3614 to 3373 BC, while later inserted burials indicated a protracted ritual significance for at least one thousand eight hundred years (Waddell 1998, 159). In relation to the cairns and possible prehistoric enclosures at Croagh Patrick, original construction dates have not been established. However, we surely find monuments that were the focus of some form of observance from prehistoric times through to modern pilgrimage today.

There is a small cluster of megalithic tombs some miles to the W of Croagh Patrick in Kilgeever parish. These consist of three court tombs and a wedge tomb, and some at least are probably representative of Late Neolithic / Early Bronze Age activity from the region. Perhaps slight parallels can be drawn between these and a group of megalithic tombs in the Dublin/Wicklow mountains where there are also a number of hilltop cairns (Grogan and Kilfeather 1997, 17-20). Surviving possible megalithic structures in our survey area are not discussed due to the uncertainty of their remains, though that at Kilsallagh Lower (6), with its well-set stones and evidence of a retaining mound, may yet take its place alongside the known megaliths in the west Mayo area.

Further monuments of a possible early date include shell middens (2-5), cairns, mounds and barrows (11-26), standing stones (27-61), ancient field fences (62-65) and fulacht fiadha (66-92). Of special significance, however, is the decorated stone at Boheh (1), located along the Togher Patrick (144), which runs westwards to the mountain. The E-W togher or routeway (144) connected Ballintubber, Co. Mayo with Croagh Patrick from Early Christian times. It is probable that this track extended farther eastwards, reaching the royal hills of Rathcroghan in Co. Roscommon where there is a pre-Christian and sacred landscape, extending back at least to early prehistoric times (Waddell 1998, 347-8). The decorated stone at Boheh heralds an important location or stop on the westward route, situated as it is on the side of the last great ridge before the final stage of the journey to the mountain mass. Whatever the origins and significance of rock art, most recent works ascribe these motifs to the same period as the creation of the megalithic tombs (Bradley 1997, 42).

Earlier in the catalogue mention was made of how Morris (1979) suggested rock art was a landmark imprint, indicative of the existence of gold in an area. Whether our knowledge of the presence of gold here was shared by our ancestors must remain open to speculation; however, their total dependence on their natural environment and their innate ability to read it, suggests that its occurrence or presence would not have escaped them. Owenwee (The Yellow River) flowing from the SW slopes of the mountain may owe its name to naturally occurring gold in the river bed. Prospectors have indeed found gold nuggets in this and other streams farther west within the past twenty years, while the presence of gold within Croagh Patrick itself is a well recognised fact today.

To date, there is no evidence for any gold mining in Ireland though the growth of bogs here may cover such signs (pers.com. Mary Cahill, National Museum). It is known that gold was worked from hard rock sources in France in the Celtic Bronze Age period (ibid.). Tests have been carried out on Irish gold artefacts and the results suggest that it is highly unlikely that Mayo was the source of the gold used in the Early Bronze Age material. Moreover, there has been insufficient work to date on the Late Bronze Age artefacts to determine if the gold originated here; however preliminary tests are not promising (ibid.).

Standing stones (27-61) of various sizes, orientation and different landscape settings occur in abundance with notable concentrations in Killeencoff (41-47) and near the seashore at Gortbraud (37, 38). Orthostats at the latter form part of a large, apparently ritual landscape, in glorious view of the mountain and at a location where the land mass of Croagh Patrick meets with the sea. A stone alignment here was curiously termed 'cromlech' on earlier O.S. maps, while in recent years it has been observed that on the shortest day of the year, the setting sun disappears in a niche in the mountain ridge, in line with it. Standing stones along the Togher Patrick (144) in Boheh (E.D. Knappagh) (27) and Lanmore (52) are taller and more pronounced than most of the others while, in size, these are similar to some tall orthostats near the coast to the west. One standing stone was located in an enclosure in Knappaghmanagh (234) which probably dates from Early Christian times, while a tentative enclosure surrounds that in Lanmore (52). The upright in Liscarney (57) was originally part of a collection of standing stones there, and may be associated with a nearby ring barrow (25). Others are located close to ringforts such as those at Cloonmonad (193), Glencally (164) and Letterbrock (217). The widely-spaced three-stone alignment at Murrisk Demesne (58) has no known association other than its location, just west of the pilgrim track to the summit from the village of Murrisk; a track whose use possibly extends back into prehistoric times. Finally, stone pairs occur at Carrowmacloughlin (30), Fahburren (33) and Letterbrock (55) while among the best sited of all orthostats is one on top of Cloonagh Hill (31).

Strictly speaking, standing stones are described as stones which were artificially placed in an upright position for a number of reasons. They may have served as grave markers, boundary signposts, or their use may have been more concerned with ceremonial or astronomical events. Uniquely, the tallest orthostat at 3.55m high was not put standing – rather it appears quarrying was carried out in a manner which left this large stone alone and upright and a most notable local landmark in Killeencoff townland.

While the particular significance of any standing stone can be difficult to determine, it is probable that they spanned a broad period of time, from at least the third millennium to the later centuries BC, and it is also probable that they had a variety of functions (Waddell 1998, 172). Their widespread use may be due to their anthropomorphic capacity and consequently their effectiveness in humanising the landscape (Tacon 1994).

Earthen burial mounds, or tumuli, and ring barrows occur in small numbers with a total of ten and three sites occurring respectively. Also included, interestingly, is a large natural mound which surely dominated the landscape of the NW slopes of the mountain since the end of the last ice age. The majority of mounds are small, 5 to 8m in diameters and 1m high on average; that in Thornhill however at 18m across and up to 2.5m high is more pronounced and set on a slight rise in a seaside field. This seaside location is shared by six others in the group (12, 14, 15, 16, 18 and 19) while two are on elevated ground overlooking Clew Bay (11, 17). In Bellataleen (11), six small unenclosed mounds 5m across and 1.2 to 1.6m high form a small possible cemetery beneath cut-away peat. Excavations throughout the country indicate that ring barrows normally date from the Iron Age, while tumuli can vary in date from as early as the Neolithic period through to the Iron Age.

Barrows tend to occur in greater numbers to the west of Louisburgh and fieldwork has shown that considerable numbers occur in the central, eastern and northern parts of the county. Two local examples (24, 25) are prominently located on ridges and all display a central mound, intervening fosse and outer bank. The tumulus cemetery at Belcarra (Raftery 1939-40), situated in low-lying flat ground, was partially excavated and produced some second millennium BC and Iron Age dates, while burials at the Carrig cemetery Co. Wicklow were dated to the late Bronze Age (Cooney and Grogen 1996, 126). A hilltop cemetery of ring barrows on Slieve Cairn near Kiltimagh extends over a wide area and commands wonderfully scenic views over much of Co. Mayo. Finally, a small group of ring barrows and tumuli together form a major complex, centred around an enormous depressed natural cavity up to 10m deep and 30m across in Carrowcloghagh, Crossmolina, Co. Mayo (sites 051 to 053 and 146, O.S. 38).

143

A total of twenty-six fulacht fiadha have been recorded with the majority likely to date to the second millennium BC. Half of these are situated on or close to the edge of flowing streams or drains with the remainder on the edge of former turloughs or damp areas. Most examples are fully intact and conform to the familiar horseshoe plan while that in Barragleanna (66) at between 150 and 185m OD is at the greatest height above sea level. Eight of the group occur in isolation, with the remainder in areas where monuments generally of a later date can be found. In most cases, some part of the site was exposed and it would appear that sandstone was exclusively used.

Radiocarbon dating of a charcoal sample from a fulacht fiadh in Knappaghbeg (87) produced a 3005 ± 110 BP date which fits it into the Bronze Age, but much earlier was the 2590-2205BC date obtained from a fulacht fiadh in Ballinrobe (Walsh 1994). While documentary sources refer to their use through the Early Christian and Medieval periods, the majority of radiocarbon dates from these sites indicate an optimum period for their creation in the middle to late Bronze Age (Brindley and Lanting 1990).

Speculation as to their function ranges from the commonly held belief that they were temporary cooking sites (O'Kelly 1954) to their possible use as saunas or sweathouses (Barfield and Hodder 1987). Their numbers around Croagh Patrick compare favourably with eleven from the Ballinrobe survey area (1989-92), twenty-two from the Belcarra Survey area (1987-88) and seven from the Mayo Abbey locality (1996).

While new examples await discovery in some of the above areas, the Turlough area of Castlebar has so far been most productive with upwards of 130 fulacht fiadha on record (Lawless 1990). Fieldwork in Turlough and more recently within The Burren, Co. Clare indicates a tendency for some fulacht fiadha to occur as small groups forming mini-clusters along a stream. With the exception of those at Brackloon (72) and Drumminaweelaun (78), this was not the case on the Croagh Patrick survey.

In summary, the most imposing of the monuments from the survey are also probably the oldest. These include the mountain cairns and perhaps the mountain summit itself (where collapsed spreads of stone from a rampart wall are all that survive). By building monuments on or close to sacred places, people perhaps believed that they could exploit the traditional significance associated with them and possibly control the access to such places (Bradley 1998, 18). This regard for sacred places may have been a feature of Irish life from Mesolithic times. The definition of places by monuments may have been primarily intended to create a sense of permanence in the relationship between communities and their environment (Cooney 2000, 129-130). Many of our standing stones are most imposing and, where concentrations occur, the possibility of further sacred sites may be anticipated. The same is true of the enduring example of rock art, which is of itself as monumental as any of the cairns. Monumentality has come to be regarded as an essential part of what being Neolithic meant in north-western Europe (Sherratt 1990; 1995a; Thomas, J. 1996a). Many of these monuments attest to a certain permanency in the early settlers and indicate considerable activity on the lower slopes of Croagh Patrick during certain periods in the Bronze Age period, at least.

A reduction in the population from the period between the close of the Bronze Age and the advent of Christianity to Ireland is suggested by the paucity of monuments from this period. The palaeoecological study in Brackloon Wood, while it cannot be representative of the entire area, suggests a decline in human activity there between about 2485 and 2005 BP (Little et al). Around the start of the fifth century AD, Ireland underwent significant change and witnessed a transformation from a static isolated society to a lively, expanding, developing and dynamic one (Mytum 1992,

7). Again, this is reflected in the pollen analysis at Brackloon Wood where an intensification of human activity is shown starting in the early centuries of the first millennium AD.

The great growth in population from the middle of the sixth century was possibly attributed to the growth of monasticism in Ireland, but also possibly due to the expansion of agriculture and horticulture and the development of more sophisticated techniques (O'Corráin 1995, 49).

Compared with isolated hermitage monasteries such at Skellig Michael, Co. Kerry and High Island, Co. Galway, the Early Christian monastic sites around Croagh Patrick are easily accessible and incapable of being cut off from their surroundings – with the obvious exception of Croagh Patrick's summit. The remainder may have served as focal points in their local communities, tending to the welfare both spiritual and religious, along with other needs of the Early Christian local population. At Oughavale (247) the establishment was so successful that it became the leading religious centre in the locality, eventually to give its name to the much later parish of Westport. At all sites except Glaspatrick (253) and Boheh (248) the monastic vallum or enclosing element is surviving. Generally speaking, locals were least aware of ecclesiastical settlements at Boheh (248) and at Fahburren (251) – at the former the land is much overgrown while a more modern private burial ground (p. 130) was the only known monument at the latter, according to most locals.

Ringforts are the predominant monument type from the Early Christian period and their presence in forty of the surveyed townlands reflects the high concentration of settlement here. Altogether a total of seventy-three ringforts were visited and local geology dictated that forty-two of these were cashels; none can compare with any of the great western stone forts as all have collapsed enclosing walls. Due to the poor preservation rate, no clear picture of the cashel wall construction technique has emerged. Original wall thickness is available at sixteen sites; of these, twelve were between 1.2m and 2m thick, with four from 2m to 2.5m thick and one of these (186) actually reached 3m in one sector. Exactly half of all cashels were constructed on substantial earth and stone foundation banks which average from 0.5m to 1m in height. While most were circular or sub-circular, a small number were more oval-shaped. Some sixteen sites provided current internal diameters of 22m or less, with the smallest one 11.7m across, located on Annagh Island (168). Very few have current internal diameters in excess of 30m while a total of twenty-one cashels are recorded whose maximum internal diameter is between 22m and 30m. Only three were enclosed by double walls though all three are very poorly preserved. Original entrances were evident at only eight sites while associated internal features were noted in fifteen cases; these consisted primarily of circular stone house foundations with a small number integrated into the cashel wall. Two souterrains are also included among the internal features. The construction of exclusively circular cashels contrasts with the Ballinrobe Survey area (1989-92), where eleven of sixty-two cashels were sub-rectangular or square, and with various parts of The Burren, Co. Clare, where nearly square cashels occur in considerable numbers. There are thirteen generally well defined raths of which the most imposing structurally is one at Carrownalurgan (189) while that with the most commanding aspect is at Rossbeg (200). In addition to these, seventeen ringforts have been recorded, and of the twenty-four enclosures visited, about half appear likely to have formed ringforts, e.g. 221, 224, 225, 226, 229, 230, 233-238.

Physical settings for the complete group of seventy-three ringforts and twelve possible ringforts are similar in many ways. All fully utilised the undulating nature of the drumlins, foothills and ridges. Most are located on slightly or well elevated land, with particularly commanding views over a 180° area. Much of the low coastal plain consists of good grazing or pasture, and forts such as those at 150, 168 and 173 appear to have taken advantage of this. In general, ringforts are plentiful throughout, apart from on the steepest slopes of the mountain and in the area covered with blanket peat to the S and SE of Croagh Patrick.

In summary, the occurrence of large numbers of ringforts is indicative of a high density of contemporary population. Their numbers within the survey area are proportionally on a par with those from more fertile parts of Co. Mayo, like Castlebar, Belcarra and Mayo Abbey, though their average diameter in size is slightly less than forts at these places.

Ringforts functioned primarily as farmsteads and the quality of surrounding lands would have provided fine grazing potential in all areas, with the additional use of rough mountain grazing for individual or common use.

Circular house foundations or hut sites have been found in association with twenty-three ringforts, while one in Glenbaun (124), partially excavated in 1992-93, showed evidence for iron working. Whether all the fifty-one examples from the area had the same function is open to debate, but it appears likely that some must simply have served as houses. In this regard, access to water was vital and twenty-five examples are located in close proximity to streams. A few, such as those at Crott Mountain (111-113), Durless (118-121), Glenbaun (125) and Glencally (115, 116) are practically on the stream's edge, and this group are additionally broader and sturdier than others in this class. The use of large facing stones in their enclosing banks gives these a fortified appearance and has also contributed to their excellent preservation. Their physical proximity to ringforts together with the Glenbaun findings suggest a possible Iron Age–Early Christian date.

Similar huts are on record from most of the archaeological surveys carried out around the country. Large numbers, primarily constructed of stone, are found on the Iveragh Peninsula (O'Sullivan & Sheehan, 1996) and the frequent use of upright slabs, reveting the inner face of their walls are also to be found in some of the better preserved local examples here. Those from the Croagh Patrick survey are all circular or sub-circular in plan while insufficient remains survive to gauge what form their roofs took. In many cases, the large build-up of stone and rubble internally could indicate corbelled buildings or clochans which collapsed inwards (e.g. 119, 125, 126). A small number of the total are conjoined huts, similar to many from the Iveragh Survey (1996).

With the exception of the friary at Murrisk (262) and the destroyed castle at Belclare (263), there is scant evidence of stone buildings from Medieval times. The remains of a later medieval church stand in the graveyard at Oughavale (247) but further buildings from this period are noticeably absent. It appears that over the centuries the presence of a church on the summit of Croagh Patrick has been one constant landmark, while it remains uncertain how many church foundations may survive on the mountain top. Likewise, it is uncertain when ecclesiastical sites such as those at Glaspatrick (253), Oughavale (247) or even Fahburren (251) became deconsecrated grounds, or when mass was last celebrated in their churches. In more recent times, a sheltered hollow in Bellataleen (called lag-an-aifreann) was reputedly a place for holding mass during the troubled Penal times. A nearby drumlin to the N (referred to locally as gallows hill) more than likely derived its name from this same troubled period.

Lazy beds or old cultivation ridges are plentiful throughout the area and can be found within both marginal and better quality land. As a rule, the lazy beds occupy the slopes of hills, ridges and drumlins in areas where even the homes of their creators have long since been removed. Many ridges probably date to around the time of the Great Famine when land utilisation was at a maximum.

Another impression on the Croagh Patrick landscape from more recent times are the large number of turf clamp bases located in certain townlands. It is not known when peat began to be harvested as a fuel source but certainly most slopes of the mountain and many of the foothills and low-lying damp pockets have today accumulated a considerable build-up of peat. During harvesting, much of the surrounding ground was damp, and stone-lined foundations were laid down to keep the turf dry, when it eventually did dry out. These foundations are rectangular in shape with one narrow side (usually facing S) unenclosed; while they occur in many of the boggy townlands, the high concentration in Bellataleen, to the east of the pilgrim track in Murrisk, is exceptional and must reflect the wet nature of that ground. Due however to the partial regeneration of heath and sphagnum, some other stone-built structures in such locations could be confused with these stone bases for turf clamps.

Throughout more recent centuries, the volume of water emanating from the mountain block was sufficient to power water mills at locations mentioned earlier (p. 140). While some were powered by large rivers such as the Owenwee (Belclare, Brackloon and Cloonagh mills) and the Bellakip (Cartoor mill), others were located on streams which would have difficulty today providing sufficient energy for such an enterprise. In this regard, the mills at Leckanvey and Bellataleen must have required a large mill pool or reservoir to maximise their power source. Few of the mills are actually located on river banks, with canalised channels or mill races showing prominently on the 1838-1844 O.S. maps. Some mills, such as that at Carrownalurgan, are barely visible, while those in Bofara, Brackloon and Cloonagh are all on major mill races diverted off the Owenwee river over considerable distances. Those in Cloonagh have a particularly well defined and deep mill race which also effectively cuts off or by-passes the semi-circular loop taken by the main river around the hilly townland of Killeencoff. Regarding stone-lined channels and sluices, those on the seashore at Belclare and Carrowkeel (Murrisk) are of most interest. Both sites today would be subjected to marine action and submerged beneath high water tides. It is known that oyster farming was carried out in the sea off Murrisk and in all probability these sluices (of timber beams and iron) were connected to this activity.

*　　*　　*

In summary, several periods are represented in monument-form throughout the survey area. A Bronze Age date of c.1000 BC from the Knappaghbeg fulacht fiadh has provided the earliest scientific date at any of the monuments. The archaeological survey has doubled the number of known antiquities locally. A more difficult challenge lies in ascribing a number of the more enigmatic sites to a chronological timeframe; in particular the Boheh rock art and the possible prehistoric remains on Croagh Patrick's summit and shoulders.

Plate 35: Early twentieth century photograph near base of the mountain, prior to the erection of St. Patrick's statue.

Chapter 6

Townland and Local Place Names

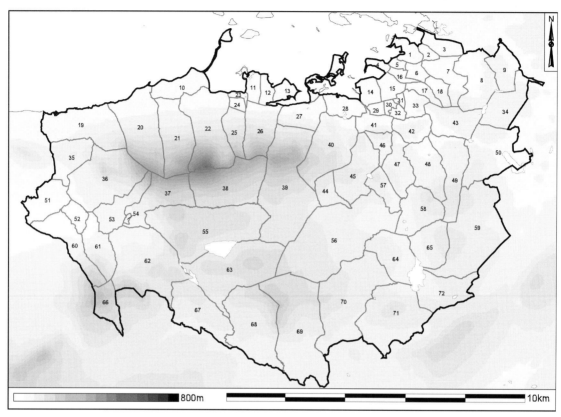

Fig 24: Survey area showing townlands. (See page opposite)

Most of our townland names today are in English or Hiberno-English, and have their roots in the Irish language. Probably the most alarming cultural change in the area over the past 150 years has been the change in the language of the people, from an exclusively Irish-speaking society to one where English is now spoken. This section deals with townland and other local place names. Some names are basic and straightforward such as Churchfield and Thornhill. Other suggestions of the meanings may be included from sources such as the Placenames Commission (Brainse Logainmneacha), O'Donovan (1838), older maps from 1638 (Petty's Atlas) and 1830 (Bald's map), all earlier O.S. maps and an 1898 Admiralty Chart. References to these places from earlier maps and their spellings then may also be included. Brief mention is given to monuments and landmarks of note from the townlands.

Ardoley *(33)*
Uncertain as to its meaning, it was tentatively suggested the height of Olaí by the Placename Commission. It contains the holy well of St. Columbkille while an old church across the main road is no longer visible; the landowner recalls evidence of the remains of this church during land reclamation. A damaged fulacht fiadh was recently detected and there is also a well preserved ringfort.

Ardmore *(2)*
The great height or hill. There is a large natural underground cavity here, referred to as a soomera. This townland contains the Quay Primary School, and there was a flour mill at the N end of Ardmore in the nineteenth century. Seventeen millstones from the mill have been dispersed throughout the Westport area.

Numerical List of Townlands

No.	Name	No.	Name	No.	Name
1	Rossbeg	26	Bellataleen	51	Mullagh
2	Ardmore	27	Deerpark West	52	Cartoor
3	Cloonmonad	28	Killadangan	53	Glenbaun
4	Rossymailley	29	Knockaraha West	54	Gorteendarragh
5	Drumminaweelaun	30	Knockaraha East	55	Barragleanna
6	Cloghan	31	Churchfield	56	Owenwee
7	Carrownalurgan	32	Aghamore	57	Tawnynameeltoge or Midgefield
8	Carrowbaun	33	Ardoley		
9	Killaghoor	34	Moyhastin	58	Boheh (Knappagh)
10	Thornhill	35	Kilsallagh Upper	59	Lanmore
11	Carrowkeel	36	Cuilleen	60	Furgill
12	Carrowkeeran	37	Glencally	61	Boheh (Kilsallagh)
13	Murrisknaboll	38	Teevenacroaghy	62	Durless
14	Belclare	39	Crott Mountain	63	Lenanadurtaun
15	Streamstown	40	Fahburren	64	Glinsk
16	Clooneen	41	Cloonagh	65	Liscarney
17	Knockfin	42	Kileencoff	66	Tangincartoor
18	Clerhaun	43	Farnaght	67	Derrymore
19	Kilsallagh Lower	44	Boleybrian	68	Pollanoughty
20	Leckanvey	45	Laghloon	69	Oughty
21	Carrowmacloughlin	46	Bofara	70	Letterbrock
22	Glaspatrick	47	Brackloon	71	Carrowrevagh
23	Murrisk Demesne	48	Knappagh More	72	Carrowmore
24	Meermihil	49	Knappagh Managh		
25	Lenacraigaboy	50	Knappagh Beg		

Aghamore *(32)*
Large or great field. A corn mill stood near S end, on a channel off the Owenwee River.

Barragleanna *(55)*
The top of the valley. Occupied by a large area of mountain and bog, it contains a well defined fulacht fiadh. Part of Lough Nacorra (the weir) lies in this townland.

Boheh *(58) & (61)*
There are two townlands by this name, and its Irish form is given as 'bothaigh' or place of many huts (Brainse Logainmneacha). Some locals prefer, both = hut and, te = hot and consequently give its origins as a sweat house. That to the E is in Aghagower parish and it contains the rock art stone, a hut site and an early ecclesiastical enclosure, while the Togher Patrick also passes through it. Some locals referred to a possible sweat house E of the Leenane road near a pond, which no longer survives.

To avoid confusion, many refer to Boheh (E.D. Kilsallagh) as Bouris, named by the Boundary Surveyor as 'Burgh'. This name is suggestive of a Medieval town settlement, as in Burrishoole or Borrisokane (O'Keane's borough town). This Boheh townland contains nine hut sites, a rath and a fulacht fiadh and the remains of a rectangular enclosure. It also contains a millstone quarry where partially worked millstones are still found. Rock outcrop on a hill in the S is called Malmore rock (big hill).

Bofara *(46)*
It may be hut of/by the sea, but it is neither close to, or in view of the sea. O'Donovan in 1838 collected the local name for it as 'hut of the prospect'. It contains one hut site. A possible English meaning is given as 'the tract of hurley playing' or 'Boc Bháire' (Brainse Logainmneacha).

Belclare *(14)*
Mouth of the plain. It contained a castle, a church and graveyard, and a bleach and corn mill, all long since gone. In more recent times, Belclare House Hotel with its outdoor heated swimming pool stood in the S of the townland. 'Balliclare' on 1683 map. A promontory in Belclare beside the mouth of the Owenwee River is named Shivdella = sibhdile meaning small projection or headland (Brainse Logainmneacha). A portion of a sluice/mill race survives in this area.

Bellataleen *(26)*
Mouth of the salt water. It runs south from the 'barrier' (local) to meet with Teevenacroaghy townland, and contains a great part of the pilgrim path which runs from Murrisk to the summit of the mountain. Monuments include one group of possible burial mounds, half a rath, one cashel and one further large stone enclosure, four fulacht fiadha, one hut site and a stone associated locally with St. Patrick. A natural drumlin beside the abandoned school house is steepest on N side and is known as 'gallows hill'. Campbell's Pub used to be the Croagh Patrick Hotel, and there was an over-shot mill located on the stream adjacent to the Tavern Bar.

Boleybrian *(44)*
Milking place or boley of Brian or the O'Briens. An uneven hilly area of no apparent antiquities.

Brackloon *(47)*
The speckled meadow; 'breac' = spotted or speckled and 'cluain' = meadow. Much of the townland is occupied by Brackloon Wood which is under the care of Coillte and receives constant environmental monitoring. There is a souterrain within a fort in the wood, with another fort on

high ground to the N where it is said young children were buried. A mill stood near the boundary with Bofara and the mill race which fed Cloonagh Mills ran through this townland. Some further smaller channels or races branch off the main river (Owenwee). It contains a destroyed group of fulacht fiadha and stones near a channel or race in the river, which were called 'the giant's grave', have been removed. A standing stone is located in Brackloon Wood.

Cahernamart

The stone fort of the oxen. Contains most of the present centre of Westport town with its wonderful architecture and street monuments. The Workhouse and Hospital stood in its W end while the railway line from Westport Station to the Quay passed through it. Monuments include a disused domestic well (Tobera Vower) and one possible fulacht fiadh.

Carrownalurgan *(7)*

The quarter of the elongated hill or ridge. Contained a coal pit in the mid-nineteenth century and has two fine raths. Local tradition maintains that there was a church in the townland, while a mill and some corn kilns were located in the NE corner.

Carrowbaun *(8)*

The white quarter. Located within its confines are two fulacht fiadha, a standing stone and two enclosures. A disused pound on the roadside has a stream flowing through it. This stream powered the mill in Carrownalurgan.

Carrowkeel *(11)*

The narrow quarter. Murrisk Friary and the former Constabulary Barracks are located here together with one cashel, one blocked-up souterrain and two other enclosures. Oyster beds and associated sluice gates are located by the seashore.

Carrowmacloughlin *(21)*

MacLoughlin's quarter. There is an enclosure with three large cairns (The Garraí Mor) on high ground, where its boundary meets with Glencally and Teevenacroaghy townlands. Everything else of archaeological interest is below an altitude of 76m and the monuments include a pair of standing stones, one burial mound, one hut site, part of a large enclosure and a lime kiln.

Carrowmore *(72)*

Large quarter. Moher (stone fort) Lake contains an impressive crannóg and otherwise the townland is home to one cashel, the remains of a large earthen enclosure, and a hut with a lime kiln built into its bank.

Churchfield *(31)*

Self-explanatory. Contained an early monastic enclosure, with the current graveyard, the remains of a medieval church and a bullaun stone all close to the road.

Cartoor *(52)*

Pronounced cortoor, the fresh hill; 'úr' = fresh, 'cor = can have several meanings, hill being one. Simply translated as 'the quarterland' (Brainse Logainmneacha). Contains three cashels, one other enclosure and a hut site. A corn kiln on the river probably accompanied the mill in this townland.

Carrowrevagh *(71)*

The grey quarter. It contains an early monastic site, a blocked-up souterrain, a rath, and a hut site on a rise.

Clerhaun (18)

O'Donovan gives it as stony ground. Flagstones of schist were quarried from the S of the townland in the last century. The Brainse Logainmneacha translate it as 'an cloichreán' (the stepping stones). It contains a well defined bivallate rath.

Cloghan (6)

Stepping stones across a river. A stream forms the townland boundary along E and much of the N. Cloghan House lies in W sector and an ancient hut nearby was landscaped with trees. Ringfort in E part.

Cloonagh (41)

Translates as a meadow. Two old flour mills and a bleach mill still survive in varying states of preservation. The Cloonagh Health Farm has re-used a later woollen mill. Close by was a tennis court while two small enclosures in the wood appear relatively modern. Turrets were incorporated into the garden wall here and one has used a millstone in its roof. Other monuments include two cashels and two further enclosures, a standing stone, and a report of a destroyed shell midden.

Clooneen (16)

A small meadow; with no known monuments.

Cloonmonad (3)

Meadow of the soft or spongy land. O'Donovan gives it as the lawn of the habitation. Stretches from The Quay to near the Leenane Road. It contains the current railway walk and the former Railway Terminus. Within Springfield Estate is a fort and a standing stone and between the railway walk and the damp ground to S is a fulacht fiadh and a well defined rath.

Crott Mountain (39)

Crott = hump. An undulating area, it contains three hut sites.

Cuilleen (36)

Little wood. 'Kelleen' in 1830. It meets with Kilsallagh Lower at the tip of Ben Goram (Gorm). Antiquities include three forts, one enclosure, four free standing huts, an enclosure and a hollowed stone bearing St. Patrick's name. A subterranean stone-built sheltered lookout from the early twentieth century was also pointed out. Part of an unfinished millstone lies on the roadside on the ascent to Lug village (lag = hollow).

Deerpark West (27)

As named. Creation of Lord Altamount and not to be confused with one nearer Westport. The townland name shows animals were kept and bred on the estate, long before the advent of Westport Zoo. This walled-in natural park contains two large enclosures for deer, or deer folds, with the entrance pillars along the main road. Two small lakes named Crott Loughs are found here with a large outcrop of rock named Carrickafoagh (the rock of the deer).

Drumminaweelaun (5)

Basically a bare ridge or hill; drummin = a hill or ridge, 'maoilín' – a little round bare hill. It contains two neighbouring fulacht fiadha and a coastal lookout turret.

Durless *(62)*

A strong fort. From 'dur' = strong and 'lios' = fort. All monuments are confined to the best land along its W border and include two good cashels (one with a souterrain) and four huts. There is a Dorlismore and a Dorlisbeg on the 1683 map with a place between them named Gortatrim; 'tromm' = the elder bush.

Fahburren *(40)*

This townland is commonly referred to as Prospect by local people.
Fahburren = either the rocky cliff if 'fall' = cliff, or the rocky level field if 'faha' or 'fa' = an exercise green. Burren is a rocky area. It contains Prospect House, former home of the Buchanan family, and a fine associated lime kiln. There was an ecclesiastical settlement near the centre of the townland with otherwise a pair of standing stones, two hut sites and a cashel to be found.

Farnaght *(43)*

An exposed hill or the hill of alder trees. An extremely rocky area, with a solitary standing stone along the S near Lettereen Lough.

Furgill *(60)*

Townland name is taken to mean 'a pledge' by O'Donovan in 1838. It contains an Early Christian monastery with a burial ground called 'Milla' (a grassy tract) and a pronounced bullaun stone. The stumps of an old pine wood grow to N and W of this site while a holy well (St. Patrick's well) lies nearby.

Glaspatrick *(22)*

St. Patrick's streamlet. Runs from the summit of the mountain to the sea. An early ecclesiastical enclosure containing a church, graveyard and holy well, along with three forts, two fulacht fiadha and an old field system are located here. The large hollow of the devil (Lugnademon) on the N face of the mountain is located in this townland.

Glenbaun *(53)*

White valley. Its antiquities include one cashel and part of a smaller enclosure, a partially excavated hut and a second hut near the cashel. Bouris School stands in this townland.

Glencally *(37)*

The glen of the marshy meadow ('cala'). It contains three cashels, one ringfort, four hut sites, one standing stone and two fulacht fiadha.

Glinsk *(64)*

Valley of the 'sceach' or thorn bush, or watery glen (Brainse Logainmneacha). Its two monuments are a cashel and a standing stone.

Gorteendarragh *(54)*

Small garden of the oak trees. The smallest townland of all, it still grows some oak. This area is referred to as 'Gortatrim' in 1683.

Killeencoff *(42)*

Small wood of the cuckoo (cuach). It contains seven standing stones, one fulacht fiadh, one cashel, one hut, an enclosure and a low burial mound. The Owenwee River encloses most of this townland.

Knappagh Beg, Knappagh Managh, Knappagh More - All townlands of small hills or hillocks (cnap). The large and small versions refer to the size of the hillocks, not the townland acreage.

Knappagh Beg *(50)*
The largest of the three contains two enclosures and the site of a fulacht fiadh. Village names include Ballinlough, Creggandarragh, Lettereen and Corranaldra.

Knappagh Managh *(49)*
(Monks) It has the remains of an early ecclesiastical enclosure where children were later buried and with a small circular hut-type feature nearby. Knappagh school house is located here. There was an enclosure or fort to the S of this containing a standing stone and souterrain.

Knappagh More *(48)*
There was an old iron mill or furnace here close to a fort. Across the road is St. Thomas' Church of Ireland, with two cashels on higher ground nearby. It also contained a corn mill near N end and a gig mill near the centre.

Kilsallagh Upper *(35)* **and Lower** *(19)*
Wood of sallow bushes or untidy wood. Spelt 'Goole Sallagh' in 1683 and 'Keilsallagh' in 1830. Kilsallagh Lower contains a possible megalithic structure, two standing stones, a cashel, a rath and a burial mound. The old National School still survives here. Kilsallagh Upper has one cashel, one ringfort and a hut.

Killadangan *(28)*
Wood of the stronghold or fortress. To S of the main road are three forts, one children's burial ground, one hut, one standing stone and one shell midden. It also contains the remains of Killadangan School, while the Post Office has long since been levelled. To N of the road is the ancient complex of monuments at Gortbraud with a cashel on the coast of Annagh (marshy) Island East. It was spelt 'Kieladangan' in 1830 and 'Cooledangan' in 1683.

Killaghoor *(9)*
Area of fresh or new woodland. Westport Railway Station is located here. It contains one enclosure, one children's burial ground, one standing stone and two fulacht fiadha.

Knockfin *(17)*
Finn (MacCool's) Hill. The possible megalithic structure within a large enclosure is called Finn MacCool's Grave. There is also a nearby hut.

Knockaraha East *(30)* **and West** *(29)*
Hill of the earthen fort (rath). The site of a fort was pointed out in Knockaraha West.

Laghloon *(45)*
Meadow of the stone heap (laght). Such a stone heap or cairn is usually of archaeological significance but such is not evident today. The only known monument in this townland consists of a standing stone near S.

Lanmore *(59)*
Large house or church. Contains one tall standing stone, three fulacht fiadha, one cashel and the remains of a turret. The reputed burial place of a priest was pointed out.

Lenacraigaboy *(25)*
The yellow stony wet meadow. There is one standing stone here.

Lenanadurtaun *(63)*
Wet meadow of tufts. One very large irregular enclosure in a boggy area is not of antiquity.

Leckanvey *(20)*
Variously translated as leac = rock or flag, of the storm (anfadh) or of Ainimhe (perhaps a personal name; Brainse Logainmneacha). Spelt 'Killcannaney' in 1683. The principal features are the village itself and the school, while formerly it housed a convent and a corn mill. It contains two burial mounds, one ringfort and another fort which was named Cahir Gall (foreign) on the 1830 map. Another mound of large proportions is named Sheeroe even today; this was spelt Shie Ruoy in 1830.

Letterbrock *(70)*
Wet hillside of the badger. It contains two enclosures, one ringfort, one cashel, a ring barrow, two standing stones, a hut and a children's burial ground. There is oral tradition of a giant's grave.

Liscarney *(65)*
Carney's lis or earthen fort. There was a corn and tuck mill and corn kilns at the river boundary with Glinsk. A millstone from that time lies on a wall at the Post Office today. Its monuments include a cashel, a ring barrow, a fulacht fiadh and a standing stone.

Meermihil *(24)*
Michael's portion (of land) (Brainse Logainmneacha). A small townland of fifty-one acres with no known antiquities.

Murrisk - Flat seaside land. There is no townland of Murrisk.

Murrisk Demesne *(23)*
It contains the National Famine Monument and Park, Murrisk Friary, a former hotel (once home to the Garvey family), three upright standing stones and two small coastal quays.

Murrisknaboll *(13)*
Sea plain of the pools or hollows. It contains an inlet name 'Polleen' and has a shell midden and burial mound. The townlands of Carrowkeel, Carrowkeeran and Murrisknaboll were all called Murrisknaboll on the 1830 map.

Moyhastin *(34)*
Hastin's plain. It contains two well defined stone forts and a ring barrow.

Mullagh *(51)*
Translates as 'the summit'. There is a hut and a bullaun stone here.

Oughty *(69)*
The breasts. Named after the two hills here. A variety of monuments are located here including one ringfort, one cashel, one rath and an enclosure containing a children's burial ground. There are also three huts, one standing stone, and a kiln-type feature containing a long subterranean flue. Some locals mentioned a group of orthostats which, however, were removed during the past fifty years.

Owenwee *(56)*

The yellow river. It contains a pre-bog field system, one hut site, a standing stone and a cashel. The name is a strong indicator of gold from the river. An area along the river at S of Crott Mountain was named Umeraree (ridge of the king) on 1830 map.

Pollanoughty *(68)*

The hollow of the hill breasts. Two cashels, a hut site, a fulacht fiadh and the remains of a handball alley are found here. A village in the S is named Cregganmore, while an area near the N boundary was interestingly named as lug-an-óir (the hollow of the gold) by O'Donovan in 1838.

Rossbeg *(1)*

Small promontory or headland. Formerly having a hotel and some salt workings, it now contains a rath on high ground and a possible shell midden by the seashore.

Rossymailley *(4)*

Promontory of the O'Malley's. A narrow promontory off the larger one has the name 'Gubnadooneen' attached to it (mouth of the small fort). No trace of a monument here or elsewhere in the townland.

Sheean (outside survey area)

The fairy hill or mound. O'Donovan states it was 'locally called Siodhan an Fháil Iartharaigh, the first land seen from the western ocean'. Contains a large built-up cairn, with a nearby circular hollowed enclosure or henge.

Streamstown *(15)*

As named. A few streams flow through or along the edges of this townland, with one along NE edge the most prominent. It contains a mound within an enclosure, a standing stone and a more recent turret.

Tangincartoor *(66)*

Could be from 'dangan' (fort or stronghold) though none could be detected. A possible meaning of tongue (projection) of the quarterland (Brainse Logainmneacha). No features of any note here.

Tawnynameeltoge *(57)*

Field of midges. No known antiquities.

Teevenacroaghy *(38)*

Side of the Reek. Ruins of old National School are still here. Upper parts have the Togher and Casán Patrick running through it, and much of the summit is in this townland also.

Thornhill *(10)*

As named. On 1830 map the name 'Cloonagh' was given to W part of the townland along the coast, while 'Knock Ribben' was applied to the area between Thornhill and Bertra. It contains a large burial mound which had a later cross erected on it to celebrate Catholic Emancipation.

The Future

Whatever the future holds, Croagh Patrick and its surrounding area certainly have a colourful past. How far back that past extends is impossible to state, yet the monuments just discussed, and the results of the palaeological study at Brackloon Wood, show active human endeavour throughout the locality from at least the Bronze Age. In keeping with other prehistoric landscapes, we find monuments here relating to the dead and their rites of passage, we find habitation and cooking sites, along with ceremonial and inauguration sites; and there is the artistically inscribed stone in Boheh, which could plausibly relate to one or more of these activities.

What has brought more people to Croagh Patrick than to any other pilgrimage site in Ireland? It is surely the close traditional connection between St. Patrick and the mountain, nurtured by the genuine belief in his having lived and prayed there for forty days. His grand pilgrimage has inspired generations of men and women of faith to follow his lofty footsteps in an attempt to strengthen that faith.

Before the arrival of Christianity to Ireland we are aware of human activity and monuments on the mountainsides, from a time at least one thousand years earlier. What is believed but cannot be proven is that the summit of the mountain was monumentalised in prehistoric times. Ironically, the popularity of the pilgrimage during the intervening millennia may have contributed to the obliteration of earlier remains on the mountain. A good indicator of pre-Christian use and practice here is the comparison drawn by Knox (1908) between Croagh Patrick and Rath Cruachan in Roscommon, as both being royal sites. Archaeologically, the collapsed wall spread enclosing the mountain's summit points to an impressive rampart wall and heightens expectations that this was indeed a strategic base or centre of power. Further excavation may be necessary to expand early dating for the area on or near the summit of Croagh Patrick.

When in 1974 the nighttime pilgrimage to Croagh Patrick was discontinued in favour of the safer daytime climbs, many felt this would spell the end for such activity, night or day. The numbers making the July pilgrimage may have been reduced, yet the numbers visiting the Reek throughout each year are increasing. Croagh Patrick became an important religious place to visit during the Early Christian and Medieval times. It is today a favoured venue for all walks of life, while still remaining a valued spiritual ascent. From hill walkers and nature lovers, photographers and civil servants, to troubled parents and budding clerics, the mountain plays host to scores of climbers with differing agendas. It is hoped that all who climb the mountain treat it with due respect. Local people have campaigned strenuously – and successfully – to ensure that gold mining is never carried out here; and locals tackle the slopes continuously to retrieve the litter abandoned by careless climbers. Croagh Patrick has survived thus far. The mountain and the people it embraces will prosper into the future; the mountain through its history, tradition and physical presence and the people, us, by the monuments, whether physical or spiritual, we leave behind.

Appendix I

List of Figures and Plates

All figures by David Loftus apart from 1a and 24 (Barry Masterson)
and 4b (courtesy of the Ordnance Survey)

Appendix II

Sponsors and Friends of Croagh Patrick

Pam & Liam Walsh, Kim & Cathal Hughes, Mary & Colm O'Neill, Patricia & James O'Doherty, Joe Berry, Jack Braiden, Dympna Benson, Michael Barrett, Olive & Des Mahon, Most Rev Michael Neary, Very Rev Padraig O'Connor, Sal & Sean Staunton, Karen & Owen Hughes, Nancy & Gordon Reid, Owen Campbell, Ann Morris, Very Rev Vincent Kelly, Pronsias Kitt, Mary & Seamus Walsh, Anne Geary, Peggy Clarke, Anne & Joe McGovern, Rose & Tony Kirby, Michael Murphy, Tommie Gill, John Mayock, Kitty O'Malley Harlow, Very Rev John Fitzgerald, Sean McDonnell, Anne Corcoran, David McDermott, Mabel & Liam Lyons, Fr Fergal Cunnane, Dr. David Cabot, Deirdre & Harry Hughes, Maura Gannon, David Lennon, Garry Kennedy, Padraic Corcoran, Paddy Hopkins, Pat & Olive Hughes, Maureen & Jackie Foley, Mary O'Flynn, Thomas J. Walsh, Very Rev Jim Walsh, Helen & Bert Farrell, Paul Barnes, Noel Golden, Alan Crean, James Likely, Mary & Tom Carr, Kevin Looby, Peter Costello, Aidan Clarke, Sr Mary Corr, Wendy & Michael Brooker, Seamus & Maria Hughes, Janet & Michael Bloor, Fr John Walsh, Cannon Tony King, Paddy Foy, Padraic Jordan, Eamonn de Burca, Bridie & Michael Moran, Mr B Foley, Bill Oakes, Breege Staunton, Richard Hughes, Joseph McKenna, Gerard O'Malley, Pearce O'Malley, Tomás P McDonough, Michael Cannon, Muintir Maigh Eo Dublin, Muintir Maigh Eo Galway, Nuala Müllan-Hughes, Brid & Pat McGing, Blanaid & John McLoughlin, Charlie Kenny, Willie Thornton, Cathal Duffy, Des Herterich, John van Wensveen, Ger Hoban, Assumpta & Pat Bree, Anna & Harry Kelly, Gerry Casey, Dan O'Neill, Tim Hastings, Peter & Maureen Flynn, Bernard O'Hara, Anne & Victor S. Wilkie, Jane & Peter Mantle, Frank Dolan, Anne & Robert Kilkelly, Francis Hughes, Peter Duffy, Kathy & Vincent Hughes, Joanne & Peter Tuohy, Vivian Kenny, Norah & Gerry Walshe, Lily & Michael Cunningham, Brother PJ Costello, Linda & Robin Smith, Teresa & Ger Reidy, Dr Finnuala Cummins, Dr Brendan Murphy, Linda & Martin Brennan, Michael & Geraldine Foy, Maureen & Brendan Byrne, Teresa & Donal Downes, Hugh Murphy, Eamon Moran, Colm Cronin, Dr Darragh Corcoran, Brendan Kealy, Jack McAleer, John Lydon, Aine & Pádraig Holland, Ray Sheehan, Prof John V Luce, Mary & Michael Cadden, Sean O'Grady, Tom Navin, Connie & Vincent Coakley, Blanaid & John Gannon, Maria Ruddy, Tony Gaughan, Declan Hughes, Pat McCormack, Peter Shanley, Geraldine & Matt Molloy, Karen & John Cox, Chris & Breda Grady, Paddy Joe Foy, Dr John Keane, Brigid & Stephen Walsh, Mary & John Groden, Patricia & Liam Gibbons, Linda & Michael McCormack, Niall Halpin, Mr & Mrs Roland Sauer, Helena & Denis Hoban, Tony & Marie O'Keeffe, Martin Beirne, Robert Kilkelly Snr., Most Rev Joseph Cassidy, Gerry & Anne Bracken, Westport UDC, Mayo County Council, South Mayo Leader Co., FÁS.

Bibliography

Books
- Barry, T.B. (1987), *The Archaeology of Medieval Ireland*, London and USA.
- Bennett, I. (various years), Bray – summary reports of excavations throughout Ireland.
  1992 – *Excavation of a small enclosure at Glenbaun, Co. Mayo* by Christine Grant and Amanda Loughran.
  1993 – *Excavation of a small enclosure at Glenbaun, Co. Mayo* by Christine Grant and Amanda Loughran. (Continuation of previous season).
  1994 – *Excavation of oratory at Glaspatrick, Croagh Patrick, Co. Mayo* by Gerry Walsh.
  1995 – *Excavation of hill-fort at Croagh Patrick/Teevenacroagh, Co. Mayo* by Gerry Walsh.
- Bradley, R. (1997), *Rock Art and the Prehistory of Atlantic Europe – Signing the Land*, London.
- Byrne, J. (ed.) (1991), *Aghaidh Achadh Mór – The Face of Aghamore*, Westport.
- Chambers, A. (1983), *Chieftain to Knight – Tibbott-ne-Long (1567-1629)*, Dublin.
- Clarke, H.B. and Ní Mhaonaigh, M. (eds.) (1998), *Ireland and Scandanavia in the Early Viking Age*, Dublin.
- Condit, E. (ed.) (1990), *Burnt Offerings* (International Contributions to Burnt Mound Archaeology, compiled by Victor Buckley), Dublin.
- Cooney, G. (2000), *Landscapes of Neolithic Ireland*, London.
- Edwards, N. (1990), *The Archaeology of Medieval Ireland*, London.
- Foster, R. F. (ed.) (1989), *The Oxford Illustrated History of Ireland,* New York containing article "Prehistoric and Early Christian Ireland", Ó Corráin (1-52).
- Harbison, P. (1998), *Pre-Christian Ireland, from the first settlers to the Early Celts*, London.
- Herity, M. and Eogan, G. (1978), *Ireland in Prehistory*, London.
- Hughes, H. (1991), *Croagh Patrick – an Ancient Mountain Pilgrimage*, Westport.
- Knox, H.T. (1908), *History of the County of Mayo*, Dublin.
- Lavelle and Jones (1994), *Ballinrobe and District*, Castlebar.
- Leask, H.G. (1966), *Irish Churches and Monastic Buildings*, Vols 1 and 3, Dundalk.
- Mallory, J. P. and McNeill, T. E. (1991), *The archaeology of Ulster*, Belfast.
- McParlan, J. (1802), *Statistical Survey of the County of Mayo*, Dublin.
- Michtell, F. (1990), *The Way that I Followed*, Dublin.
- Mytum, H. (1992), *The Origins of Early Christian Ireland*, London.
- O'Croinín, D. (1995), *Early Medieval Ireland*, London.
- O'Hara, B. (1982), *Mayo – Aspects of its Heritage*, Galway.
- O'Sullivan, A. and Sheehan, J. (1996*), The Iveragh Peninsula – an Archaeological Survey of South Kerry*, Cork.
- Ordnance Survey Field Name Books of the County of Mayo Books (1838), *Parish of Oughaval*, 59 and 60, Parts 1 and 2 respectively, Dublin.
- Ottway, C. (1839), *A tour in Connaught comprising sketches of Clonmacnoise, Joyce country and Achill,* Dublin.
- Subolewski, P. and Solan, B. (eds.) (1996), *Kiltimagh – Our life and times*, Dublin.
- Sweetman, D. (1999), *The Medieval Castles of Ireland*, Cork.
- The Marquess of Sligo (1981), *Westport House and the Brownes*, Derbyshire.
- Waddell, J. (1998), *The Prehistoric Archaeology of Ireland*, Galway University Press.

Journals and limited copies
1. J.G.A.H.S. Vol. 19, 1940, 16-89.
   "The Tumulus Cemetery of Carrowjames, Co. Mayo". Joseph Raftery M.A. Dr. Phil.
2. J.G.A.H.S. Vol. 18, 1939, 157-167.
   "The Tumulus Cemetery of Carrowjames, Co. Mayo". Joseph Raftery M.A. Dr. Phil.
3. "Archaeological Excavations on the Ballinrobe Sewage and Sewerage Disposal Scheme 1994". Gerry Walsh, 1994.

Biobliography (continued) . . .

4. "Archaeological Excavations on the Swinford Bypass N5". Gerry Walsh, 1993.
5. 'A Palaeological Study of Brackloon Wood, Co. Mayo' (unpublished). Vegetation Dynamics and Human Impact throughout the Holocene Period (c. 10,000 years BP – present) Feb. 2000. S. von Engelbrechten, E. McGee, D.J. Little and F.J.G. Mitchell.
6. "500 years in the History of Murrisk Abbey". Pádraig O'Móráin M.A. (Mayo News) 1957.
7. Mayo Abbey Survey (unpublished). Leo Morahan, 1996, in Mayo Co. Library, Castlebar.
8. Cathair na Mart – Journal of the Westport Historical Society (for various articles)
    -   No. 1 (Vol. 1), 1981. Sheila Mulloy. 'Some 17th century links with Brittany.'
    -   No. 1 (Vol. 7), 1987, p. 32-36. Victor M. Buckley and Christy Lawless. 'Prehistoric cooking in Co. Mayo.'
    -   No. 1 (Vol. 8), 1988, p. 23-25. Victor M. Buckley and Christy Lawless. 'Two carbon 14 dates for fulachta fiadha at Turlough, near Castlebar.'
    -   No. 1 (Vol. 10), 1990, p. 1-10. Christy Lawless. 'A fulacht fiadh Bronze Age cooking experiment at Turlough, Castlebar.'
    -   No. 12, 1992, p. 1-12, G.G. Bracken and P.A. Wayman. 'A Neolithic or Bronze Age alignment for Croagh Patrick.'
    -   No. 13, 1993, p. 1-15. Maarten van Hoek. 'The prehistoric Rock Art of the Boheh Stone.'
    -   No. 14, 1994, p. 1-11. Gerry Walsh. 'Preliminary report on the archaeological excavations on the summit of Croagh Patrick, 1994.'
    -   No. 15, 1995, p. 15-25. Maarten van Hoek. 'The Keyhole Pattern in the prehistoric Rock Art of Ireland and Britain.'
9. J.R.S.I. 32 (1902), 132-138.
    "Occupation of Connacht by the Anglo-Normans after AD 1237". H.T. Knox.
10. Mac Gabhaun T. (ed.) 1990, in Carloviana (Journal of the Old Carlow Society) "Deerparks". Gibbons M. & Clarke T, 4-5.
11. J.I.A. IX (1998), 45-63.
    "Radiocarbon Dates for Irish Trackways". Brindley A.L. & Lanting J.N.
12. J.I.A. IX (1998), 9-26.
    "The Prehistoric Ritual Landscape of Croagh Patrick, Co. Mayo". Christiaan Corlett.
13. "An Archaeological Survey of the Basin of the River Deel, Co. Mayo". Keane M. 1989, Vol. I (unpublished).
14. Letters containing information relative to the antiquities of the County of Mayo, collected during the progress of the Ordnance Survey in 1838, Vol. I. 1927, Bray.

*   *   *

-   A map of the Maritime County of Mayo, in 25 sheets, commenced in 1809 and terminated in 1817, by William Bald F.R.S.E. Printed in 1830.
-   Hiberniae Delineatio Atlas of Ireland by Sir William Petty, 1685, Newcastle Upon Tyne.
-   Six inch Ordnance Survey Maps of 1838-44, 1901, 1919, 1920, 1921 and 1929.
-   Sites and Monuments Record – Archaeological Constraint Maps, September 1996.
-   Map published according to Act of Parliament at the Hydrographic Office on the Admiralty, May 30, 1851 and revised 1898.

Front Cover:
Panoramic view of a cashel in Knappaghmore (176) with Croagh Patrick in the background – *Leo Morahan*
Back Cover Collage:
Murrisk Friary, souterrain in Durless, and Mr. Austin Moran R.I.P., Killeencoff – *Leo Morahan*
Bertra Beach – *Michael O'Sullivan*
Statue of Saint Patrick – *Harry Hughes*
Pilgrims in Murrisk, circa 1905 – *Harry Hughes Collection*

Index

Index: continued